AI and Machine Learning in Procurement

Strategies for Modern Sourcing

AI and Machine Learning in Procurement

Part 1: Introduction to AI and Machine Learning in Procurement

Chapter 1: The Evolution of Procurement Technology

Procurement has come a long way from being a simple, tactical function focused on obtaining goods and services at the lowest possible cost. Today, it is a strategic driver of organizational value, supported by cutting-edge technologies, including AI and machine learning (ML). This chapter explores the phases that procurement technology has traversed, charting a course from early rudimentary methods to modern AI-powered solutions that are reshaping how businesses source, purchase, and manage supplier relationships.

1. The Beginnings of Procurement: Manual Processes and Documentation

In its initial form, procurement was largely a manual process. Procurement professionals relied on handwritten records, paper-based requisitions, and phone or in-person negotiations to fulfill organizational purchasing needs. Key considerations were price, availability, and timely delivery, with procurement managers balancing quality and cost in sourcing goods and services. This period relied heavily on relationships with suppliers and a deep understanding of available resources.

The limitations of manual methods became evident as organizations expanded and supply chains grew more complex. Tracking spending, negotiating contracts, and maintaining supplier relationships all relied on human memory and physical records, leading to inefficiencies and errors. Any attempts at performance analysis or demand forecasting were difficult to achieve accurately, and information silos restricted collaboration across departments.

2. Early Digitization: The Rise of Basic Procurement Software

The 1980s and 1990s introduced a wave of digitization across industries, including procurement. Basic enterprise resource planning (ERP) systems began to include procurement functions, enabling digital record-keeping, basic spend analysis, and automated workflows. This shift from paper to digital documentation marked a fundamental change in procurement operations, allowing for more efficient data management, improved organization, and better visibility across supply chain functions.

During this era, spreadsheets became indispensable for tracking purchases and budgets. While helpful, they were still labor-intensive, and the data inputs required were often manual. However, these tools

7

laid the foundation for greater data centralization, which would become instrumental as procurement technology advanced. The automation of routine tasks began to save valuable time and reduce human error, making the procurement process slightly more efficient but still dependent on significant manual input.

Key Technologies of This Era:

Early ERP systems with basic procurement functionality.

Spreadsheet software, primarily Excel, for data tracking and analysis.

Digital documentation for order processing and contract management.

3. The Automation Wave: Integrated Procurement Systems and Strategic Sourcing

The turn of the millennium ushered in more sophisticated procurement solutions. Organizations began to recognize procurement's strategic potential, leading to the development of more advanced tools to support not only transactional activities but also strategic sourcing, supplier relationship management, and contract lifecycle management. The advent of e-procurement systems, which allowed companies to conduct purchasing processes online, was a major turning point. These systems enabled greater transparency, data access, and integration with other business functions.

E-procurement solutions introduced digital catalogues, automated purchase order creation, and approval workflows. With automation capabilities, procurement professionals could manage more significant volumes of data and execute processes more quickly and accurately than before. Strategic sourcing—emphasizing total cost of ownership over mere price—emerged as a core procurement focus. Data analysis became a vital part of decision-making, supported by software that could generate insights on supplier performance, contract compliance, and spending trends.

Key Technologies of This Era:

E-procurement platforms, streamlining and digitizing procurement processes.

Contract lifecycle management (CLM) systems.

Supplier relationship management (SRM) software.

Spend analysis tools that allowed for deeper insights into procurement data.

4. Data-Driven Procurement: Big Data, Advanced Analytics, and Cloud Solutions

By the 2010s, the explosion of data in procurement and supply chain management led to the adoption of more advanced analytics. Big data solutions allowed companies to leverage large datasets from multiple sources—such as internal transactions, supplier databases, and market intelligence—to make more informed and accurate procurement decisions. This era also saw a migration to cloud-based platforms, which provided real-time data access, scalability, and the ability to share information seamlessly across locations.

Cloud-based procurement solutions offered a new level of flexibility, allowing procurement teams to collaborate globally, access information on-demand, and work with advanced analytical tools without the need for extensive on-premises infrastructure. Real-time data availability improved decision-making and responsiveness to changing market conditions, while advanced analytics tools allowed procurement teams to predict demand, optimize inventory, and reduce supply chain risks. The focus on data-driven insights transformed procurement from a cost center into a value-generating function, capable of supporting company-wide objectives.

Key Technologies of This Era:

Cloud-based procurement platforms, improving data accessibility and collaboration.

Big data analytics, allowing for predictive insights into demand and supplier performance.

Internet of Things (IoT), enabling real-time tracking of inventory and shipments.

Enhanced cybersecurity, critical for protecting sensitive procurement data.

5. The AI-Driven Revolution in Procurement

The integration of artificial intelligence and machine learning into procurement is a recent development, but one that has already made a profound impact. These technologies go beyond automation and analysis by adding cognitive capabilities that enable predictive insights, autonomous decision-making, and intelligent automation. AI and ML offer procurement teams the power to not only streamline processes but to generate actionable insights from vast datasets, allowing for deeper visibility into spending patterns, supplier performance, and risk factors.

Machine learning models are particularly valuable for demand forecasting, risk assessment, and spend analysis, as they can identify patterns and trends in data that traditional analytics may miss. AI-powered platforms can analyze supplier histories, market conditions, and contractual terms to recommend the best sourcing options, predict price fluctuations, and flag potential risks. Natural language processing (NLP) enables sentiment analysis in supplier interactions and improves contract management by automating the extraction and interpretation of contract terms.

This era has expanded the boundaries of procurement, enabling organizations to transition from reactive to proactive, data-informed decision-making. AI and ML applications have brought procurement closer to the heart of strategic business decision-making by aligning it with key organizational objectives like cost reduction, sustainability, and risk mitigation.

Key Technologies of This Era:

AI and ML for predictive insights, process automation, and risk management.

Natural language processing (NLP) for contract and supplier sentiment analysis.

Autonomous procurement solutions, allowing for self-governing processes.

Blockchain technology, adding transparency and security to supply chain data.

6. Benefits and Challenges of Evolving Procurement Technology

The evolution of procurement technology has delivered numerous benefits, including cost savings, process efficiency, and data visibility. However, these advancements come with challenges. The rapid pace of technological change requires continuous learning and adaptation for procurement teams. Data privacy concerns, ethical considerations in AI usage, and the risk of technological disruptions are critical issues that organizations must address to maximize the value of these tools.

7. The Road Ahead: AI and the Future of Procurement

Looking forward, AI and ML are likely to play an even more transformative role in procurement. As these technologies mature, they will allow for more sophisticated automation, seamless supplier collaboration, and enhanced risk management. Procurement will move further into predictive and prescriptive analytics, enabling organizations to anticipate needs and make data-informed decisions proactively.

Future advancements may include autonomous procurement agents, real-time negotiations, and AI-driven recommendations for supplier diversity and sustainability initiatives. As AI becomes more integrated into procurement processes, organizations must be prepared to manage the ethical, privacy, and security implications of its use.

The evolution of procurement technology reflects a journey from basic manual methods to a sophisticated, AI-driven ecosystem. This progression highlights the transition of procurement from a back-office function to a strategic enabler of business value. Through each phase, procurement has harnessed new technologies to improve efficiency, accuracy, and decision-making. Today, AI and ML stand at the forefront, driving procurement into a future where innovation, agility, and strategic foresight will define its role in organizational success.

By understanding this evolution, procurement professionals can better appreciate the potential of AI and ML to transform their field, positioning them to leverage these tools to drive measurable impact and competitive advantage in an increasingly complex global landscape.

This overview offers a rich foundation, with each phase adding to the narrative of procurement's transformation over time. Let me know if you need further elaboration on any specific aspect, or if you'd like to explore additional sections like case studies or practical applications in this chapter.

Chapter 2: Understanding AI and Machine Learning Fundamentals

In this chapter, we'll establish a foundational understanding of artificial intelligence (AI) and machine learning (ML), with a focus on applications specifically relevant to procurement. We'll cover AI and ML's basic concepts, how these technologies differ, and how they're used to drive innovation, efficiency, and strategic decision-making in procurement.

AI and ML are no longer futuristic technologies; they are part of our everyday digital interactions, from voice-activated assistants to targeted advertisements. In procurement, AI and ML provide the analytical depth needed to handle vast data volumes, improve efficiency, and support informed, strategic decisions. This chapter offers an introductory look at AI and ML, key distinctions between the two, and their relevant applications within procurement.

1. What is Artificial Intelligence?

Artificial intelligence refers to machines designed to mimic human intelligence, capable of learning, reasoning, problem-solving, and even perceiving environmental conditions. AI's goal is to enable systems to perform complex tasks that traditionally required human intelligence. AI capabilities range from recognizing patterns in data to making decisions based on historical knowledge, predictive modeling, and real-time information.

In procurement, AI is primarily used for analyzing data at an unprecedented scale, identifying patterns that would otherwise go unnoticed, and delivering predictive insights. For example, AI can analyze purchasing trends to forecast demand, anticipate price fluctuations, and evaluate supplier performance. This capacity allows procurement professionals to shift from reactive to proactive and even prescriptive strategies, where AI systems can recommend optimal actions.

2. The Basics of Machine Learning: The Core of AI

Machine learning is a subset of AI and is at the heart of many AI applications. ML involves algorithms that improve their performance by learning from data. Rather than being explicitly programmed to perform every task, ML models use data to train themselves to recognize patterns, make decisions, or predict outcomes. In procurement, ML applications analyze past data to forecast demand, optimize inventory, classify suppliers, and assess risk.

There are three main types of machine learning approaches, each with relevance to procurement:

Supervised Learning: In supervised learning, the algorithm is trained on labeled data, where each input is paired with an output. In procurement, supervised learning models might use historical purchase data to forecast demand for different products based on factors like season, market trends, and past sales.

Unsupervised Learning: Here, the algorithm is trained on data without labeled outputs, allowing it to discover patterns on its own. For instance, unsupervised learning can group suppliers based on behavior, pricing patterns, or risk factors, helping procurement managers identify unique supplier segments.

Reinforcement Learning: This is a feedback-based learning method where algorithms learn by receiving rewards for correct actions and penalties for incorrect ones. Reinforcement learning can optimize procurement decisions by simulating various scenarios and identifying the strategies that yield the best outcomes over time.

3. Key Concepts and Terminology in AI and ML for Procurement

Understanding the terminology used in AI and ML can help procurement professionals better appreciate these technologies' role in their work. Below are some critical terms:

Algorithms: Algorithms are sets of rules or instructions that a machine uses to process data and make decisions. Algorithms in ML are designed to find patterns, classify data, or predict outcomes.

Neural Networks: These are layers of algorithms designed to mimic the way the human brain processes information. Neural networks are essential in deep learning, which is used for complex data analysis tasks in procurement, such as analyzing supplier sentiment.

Natural Language Processing (NLP): NLP is the field of AI focused on enabling computers to understand, interpret, and generate human language. In procurement, NLP is used in contract analysis, where algorithms can extract key clauses, identify risks, and summarize contract terms efficiently.

Predictive Analytics: This refers to using historical data and algorithms to make predictions about future events. In procurement, predictive analytics can forecast demand, supplier reliability, and potential risks, enabling more proactive decision-making.

Data Mining: Data mining is the process of discovering patterns and relationships in large datasets. In procurement, data mining is often used to analyze spending data, identify cost-saving opportunities, and optimize supplier selection.

4. How AI and ML Differ from Traditional Data Analytics

Traditional data analytics tools rely on structured, historical data and predefined rules. While they can be powerful, they are often limited in scope and unable to adapt to new data inputs or make decisions beyond their programming. AI and ML, in contrast, can learn from data in real time, adapt to new patterns, and generate insights that aren't limited to pre-programmed rules.

For example, a traditional analytics tool in procurement might analyze quarterly spending data and generate a report, whereas an AI-powered tool could continuously monitor spending, flag irregularities as they arise, and even recommend corrective actions in real-time. This adaptive capability makes AI and ML ideal for fast-paced environments where conditions can change rapidly, such as in supply chain and procurement.

5. Key Applications of AI and ML in Procurement

AI and ML can significantly improve procurement by automating tasks, enhancing decision-making, and providing strategic insights. Here are some of the most impactful applications:

A. Demand Forecasting

Accurate demand forecasting is crucial for effective procurement. Traditional methods often fall short in predicting demand changes due to market shifts, seasonal patterns, or external factors like economic trends. ML algorithms can analyze vast data volumes, including historical sales, seasonal data, and external market indicators, to create highly accurate demand forecasts. These models can adapt to changes, helping procurement teams manage inventory, reduce stockouts, and minimize excess stock.

B. Supplier Selection and Evaluation

Selecting and evaluating suppliers is a complex task involving multiple criteria such as price, quality, reliability, and compliance. AI-powered platforms can assess suppliers based on structured and unstructured data, such as performance records, reviews, and financial stability. ML algorithms can rank suppliers, predict potential risks, and recommend the best choices based on comprehensive data analysis. These insights enable procurement professionals to make more strategic, data-driven supplier decisions.

C. Spend Analysis and Cost Optimization

Spend analysis is one of the core functions of procurement, aimed at understanding where and how money is being spent. AI can automate the categorization of spending data, identify savings opportunities, and detect irregularities. Machine learning models can also forecast budget requirements, assess cost trends, and help in negotiating better terms with suppliers by analyzing pricing and spending patterns.

D. Risk Management

AI can be instrumental in mitigating risks associated with procurement. Machine learning models can evaluate supplier risk by analyzing a variety of factors, including performance history, financial health, market stability, and geopolitical conditions. Predictive analytics can identify emerging risks before they become issues, allowing procurement teams to proactively adjust sourcing strategies. Additionally, AI can monitor regulatory compliance and flag any transactions or suppliers that may pose legal or reputational risks.

E. Contract Management

Procurement contracts contain a wealth of data but are often cumbersome to manage and analyze manually. NLP, a subset of AI, can extract critical information from contracts, such as terms, clauses, and deadlines. By automating contract analysis, AI helps procurement teams quickly identify risks, ensure compliance, and avoid penalties due to missed deadlines or breaches of terms. This automation also reduces the administrative burden, freeing procurement professionals to focus on strategic tasks.

F. Automation of Routine Procurement Tasks

Procurement involves numerous repetitive tasks, such as purchase orders, invoice processing, and data entry. Automating these tasks through AI improves efficiency, reduces errors, and allows procurement professionals to dedicate more time to strategic activities. For example, AI-driven robotic process automation (RPA) can handle routine tasks in the procurement workflow, enabling faster and more accurate processes without human intervention.

6. Benefits of AI and ML in Procurement

The integration of AI and ML offers several strategic advantages:

Improved Efficiency: Automation and predictive capabilities streamline operations, saving time and reducing errors.

Enhanced Decision-Making: AI and ML analyze vast datasets to generate insights that support data-driven, strategic decisions.

Cost Savings: AI-powered spend analysis and cost optimization help organizations reduce procurement costs and manage budgets more effectively.

Risk Mitigation: Predictive analytics and risk assessment tools help identify and mitigate potential risks, ensuring a more secure supply chain.

Greater Agility: AI allows procurement teams to respond quickly to market changes, demand fluctuations, and supply disruptions.

7. Challenges of Implementing AI and ML in Procurement

While AI and ML bring significant benefits, there are challenges:

Data Quality and Availability: AI and ML models rely on quality data, which can be difficult to obtain or integrate across systems.

Skills Gap: Many procurement teams may lack the technical skills needed to manage and interpret AI-driven insights.

Cost of Implementation: Developing and implementing AI solutions can be costly, particularly for smaller organizations.

Ethical and Privacy Concerns: AI applications must be carefully managed to avoid issues related to privacy, bias, and ethical use of data.

8. The Path Forward for AI in Procurement

As AI and ML continue to advance, their applications in procurement will become more sophisticated. Future developments may include autonomous procurement agents, real-time negotiations powered by AI, and advanced supplier diversity and sustainability tools. By understanding AI and ML fundamentals, procurement professionals can be better prepared to leverage these technologies for strategic advantage, ensuring that procurement remains a value-driving function within the organization.

This chapter sets the stage for more specific AI applications in procurement, helping readers grasp the basics of AI and ML and appreciate their transformative potential. Let me know if you'd like further detail on any specific section or application.

Chapter 3: The Role of AI in Modern Procurement

In recent years, artificial intelligence (AI) has emerged as a transformative force in procurement, reshaping how organizations source, manage suppliers, and make decisions. Modern procurement is no longer just about finding the lowest price but about building resilient, responsive, and strategic supply chains. AI enables procurement to move beyond traditional, manual processes and reactive decision-making to embrace a data-driven, predictive, and proactive approach. This chapter explores AI's role in modern procurement, from automating routine tasks to enabling strategic decision-making, enhancing supplier relationships, and driving efficiencies across the procurement process.

As the world becomes increasingly data-driven, procurement departments are being challenged to keep up with market complexities, operational speed, and dynamic risk factors. The integration of AI in procurement is a solution to these challenges, providing tools that analyze data at scale, uncover valuable insights, and support decisions that align with an organization's strategic goals. Let's look into how AI is reshaping procurement processes and decision-making in detail.

1. Automating Routine Procurement Processes

AI's automation capabilities are one of its most immediate impacts in procurement. Procurement workflows often include repetitive, manual tasks like purchase order management, invoice processing, and data entry. These tasks, while essential, are time-consuming and prone to human error. AI-powered automation tools can handle these tasks quickly and accurately, freeing procurement professionals to focus on higher-value work.

For example, robotic process automation (RPA), often enhanced by AI algorithms, can handle repetitive tasks, manage data migration, and process purchase requests autonomously. This reduces the likelihood of errors, improves process efficiency, and ultimately cuts down on administrative costs. By automating these processes, procurement can operate more smoothly and adapt to fluctuating volumes without increasing headcount.

2. Enhancing Decision-Making with Data-Driven Insights

One of AI's most transformative contributions to procurement is in enabling data-driven decision-making. AI can process and analyze large volumes of data from various sources—supplier performance, market trends, historical purchasing data, and external economic indicators—to generate insights that inform decision-making.

For instance, AI algorithms can detect patterns in spend data, identify trends in supplier performance, and highlight areas where costs can be optimized. This capability shifts procurement from reactive problem-solving to proactive decision-making, where decisions are based on real-time and predictive data. AI's data-processing power also enables procurement teams to perform "what-if" analyses, which simulate different scenarios to forecast the impact of various decisions, helping organizations prepare for a range of market conditions.

3. Supplier Relationship Management (SRM) and Supplier Evaluation

Supplier relationships are critical to procurement's success, and AI can add value in this area by helping procurement teams evaluate and manage suppliers more effectively. Through predictive analytics and machine learning, AI can analyze supplier data—such as delivery performance, quality metrics, financial health, and compliance records—to provide a comprehensive view of each supplier's reliability and potential risks.

Additionally, AI can monitor ongoing supplier performance in real time, flagging issues such as delays or quality concerns before they become major problems. This level of transparency and oversight allows procurement to maintain stronger relationships with strategic suppliers while identifying potential risks in the supply chain. Moreover, by using natural language processing (NLP) to analyze supplier contracts and external reports, AI can evaluate suppliers' adherence to contractual terms and extract insights from unstructured data sources such as news articles, reviews, and financial reports.

4. Risk Management and Predictive Risk Analysis

Managing risks—whether they are financial, operational, or geopolitical—has always been a core function of procurement. AI enhances risk management in procurement by providing predictive insights that allow organizations to anticipate and mitigate risks more effectively. Traditional risk management methods often rely on historical data and tend to be reactive. In contrast, AI can continuously analyze a multitude of risk indicators, such as supplier performance, market volatility, or regulatory changes, to predict risks before they materialize.

For example, AI can assess a supplier's risk of default by analyzing data points like their credit rating, delivery performance, and financial health. Additionally, AI-driven risk analysis can highlight broader risks in the supply chain, such as those posed by political instability or extreme weather patterns in key sourcing regions. This predictive capability gives procurement teams a proactive edge, enabling them to secure alternate suppliers or adjust sourcing strategies as necessary to protect supply continuity.

5. Spend Analysis and Cost Optimization

Spend analysis and cost optimization are fundamental objectives in procurement, and AI-driven tools excel at delivering insights that support these goals. Traditional spend analysis can be labor-intensive and often lacks the agility to adapt to rapidly changing data. AI can analyze spend data continuously and in real time, identifying patterns, cost-saving opportunities, and inefficiencies that would otherwise go unnoticed.

For instance, AI can automatically categorize spending data across departments or product categories, regardless of inconsistencies in data entry. It can also identify instances where procurement deviates from preferred supplier agreements, flagging opportunities for renegotiation or cost reduction. By providing a granular, up-to-date view of spending

24

across the organization, AI allows procurement teams to drive cost savings through better visibility and informed decision-making.

6. Demand Forecasting and Inventory Optimization

Accurate demand forecasting is crucial for procurement to optimize inventory levels, reduce stockouts, and minimize excess stock. AI-powered demand forecasting models are capable of incorporating multiple data points—historical sales, seasonality, economic trends, and even social media trends—to generate highly accurate forecasts. Unlike traditional forecasting models, which may rely on limited historical data, AI-based forecasting tools can adapt to new data inputs and dynamically update forecasts based on real-time information.

This capability has far-reaching benefits for procurement. By accurately predicting demand, organizations can plan their purchasing more strategically, order in economically advantageous quantities, and avoid costly last-minute purchases or emergency stockouts. AI-driven forecasting also enhances supplier collaboration, as suppliers benefit from better visibility into demand projections and can plan their production schedules accordingly.

7. Contract Management and Compliance

Contract management is an area of procurement that is both time-intensive and prone to risk if not handled correctly. AI offers solutions for managing and analyzing contracts efficiently. Using natural language processing (NLP), AI can review contracts, extract key information such as payment terms, delivery schedules, and compliance clauses, and even assess contracts for potential risks or discrepancies.

AI-powered contract management tools can automatically track contract milestones, monitor compliance, and flag upcoming deadlines.

This reduces the risk of missed obligations or breaches, which can result in penalties or strained supplier relationships. By automating contract review and analysis, procurement teams save time, ensure compliance, and reduce administrative burdens.

8. Enhancing Procurement's Agility and Responsiveness

In today's fast-paced market environment, procurement needs to be agile and responsive to sudden changes in demand, supplier availability, or market conditions. AI enables this agility by providing real-time insights and automating workflows that would traditionally take days or weeks to process. For example, if a sudden supply chain disruption occurs, AI tools can quickly assess the situation, identify alternative suppliers, and adjust order quantities based on revised demand forecasts.

This agility is critical not only for maintaining supply continuity but also for capitalizing on market opportunities. AI's ability to generate real-time insights and facilitate rapid response actions ensures that procurement remains a strategic, value-adding function rather than a bottleneck in the organization.

9. Strategic Supplier Diversity and Sustainability Initiatives

In response to increasing demands for ethical and sustainable sourcing, many organizations are prioritizing supplier diversity and sustainability in procurement. AI can support these initiatives by analyzing supplier data related to environmental, social, and governance (ESG) metrics, helping procurement teams assess which suppliers align with their corporate values.

For example, AI-powered tools can evaluate suppliers' carbon footprints, waste management practices, and labor policies, providing a quantifiable basis for supplier selection. By leveraging these insights, procurement can prioritize suppliers that meet sustainability criteria, support corporate social responsibility goals, and enhance the organization's reputation with consumers and stakeholders.

10. Building a Strategic Advantage with AI in Procurement

AI is helping transform procurement from a back-office function into a strategic asset. By leveraging AI's capabilities, procurement can drive competitive advantage through cost savings, efficiency, risk mitigation, and better supplier management. With AI, procurement teams can harness data to identify opportunities, make proactive decisions, and align their objectives with the organization's broader strategic goals.

AI also supports the shift toward "cognitive procurement," where procurement functions move beyond data analysis to incorporate strategic insights, predictive models, and even autonomous decision-making. By integrating AI, procurement can elevate its role within the organization, becoming a source of competitive advantage that directly contributes to the company's success.

In this chapter, we have explored the multifaceted role of AI in modern procurement, covering how it automates tasks, enhances decision-making, manages supplier relationships, and ensures compliance. By understanding and leveraging AI, procurement teams can maximize efficiency, improve resilience, and contribute strategically to organizational objectives. This marks the beginning of a new era in procurement, where AI will continue to push boundaries and drive innovation.

Chapter 4: Machine Learning vs. Traditional Procurement Methods

As the procurement landscape becomes more complex and data-driven, organizations are increasingly recognizing the limitations of traditional methods. While conventional procurement approaches have been effective for decades, they rely heavily on manual data analysis, fixed historical trends, and experience-based judgment. In contrast, machine learning (ML) brings advanced predictive capabilities, adaptability, and automation that allow procurement teams to operate more efficiently, make data-driven decisions, and respond proactively to market dynamics.

Procurement teams today face dynamic supply chain challenges that demand speed, accuracy, and insight. Traditional procurement methods, which rely on historical data, manual analysis, and fixed rules, often struggle to keep up with these requirements. Machine learning (ML) offers an alternative by providing predictive insights, real-time adaptability, and continuous learning capabilities. Let's examine how ML differs from traditional procurement methods and the impact it is having on modern procurement.

1. Data Processing and Analysis: Static vs. Dynamic

In traditional procurement, data analysis relies on historical data and periodic reviews, with procurement professionals analyzing purchase orders, supplier performance, and cost trends manually or through simple rule-based systems. These conventional approaches use static models, where predictions are based on past data without accounting for rapid changes in demand, supply, or market conditions.

Machine learning, on the other hand, excels in processing vast datasets continuously and in real time. ML algorithms can detect patterns, identify correlations, and adjust forecasts based on the latest data, creating a dynamic approach to data analysis. This enables ML-driven systems to make predictions that are not only based on historical trends but are also updated as new data becomes available. For example, an ML model can adjust its forecast based on current economic indicators, weather patterns, or recent shifts in consumer behavior, giving procurement teams a more accurate and timely picture.

2. Demand Forecasting and Inventory Management

Traditional procurement forecasting methods often rely on historical demand data, seasonal patterns, and manual trend analysis to estimate future needs. While this approach can be effective, it may miss subtleties in demand fluctuations or fail to respond to unexpected changes, leading to stockouts or excess inventory.

Machine learning transforms demand forecasting by utilizing real-time data inputs and predictive algorithms. ML models can process large and diverse datasets, including social media trends, economic forecasts, and customer purchasing behaviors, to predict demand with a high degree of accuracy. Additionally, ML algorithms can adapt as new data comes in, allowing forecasts to adjust dynamically in response to external changes. This adaptability ensures that inventory levels are optimized, reducing costs associated with overstocking or emergency stock replenishment.

For example, an ML-driven forecasting tool might identify an upcoming spike in demand based on social media sentiment or weather patterns. This proactive approach allows procurement teams to plan for demand more effectively than traditional forecasting methods, which would have only considered past seasonal trends.

3. Supplier Evaluation and Selection: Manual vs. Automated Analysis

Supplier evaluation in traditional procurement is often a lengthy, manual process. Procurement professionals assess suppliers based on performance metrics, historical reliability, and compliance with contractual terms. This manual analysis, while thorough, can be time-consuming and may overlook subtle indicators of risk or performance variability.

Machine learning simplifies and enhances supplier evaluation by automating the analysis of supplier data. ML algorithms can evaluate suppliers based on numerous variables, such as delivery performance, quality scores, and financial health, often going beyond what is possible in manual analysis. Furthermore, ML models can detect early warning signs of potential supplier issues, such as declining performance trends or financial instability, allowing procurement teams to mitigate risks proactively.

An ML-driven supplier evaluation system might flag a supplier that, although compliant in recent assessments, shows signs of financial distress based on trends in external data sources (e.g., news reports, financial filings). By identifying such risks early, procurement can make more informed decisions about which suppliers to engage, contributing to a more resilient and reliable supply chain.

4. Spend Analysis and Cost Optimization

Traditional spend analysis typically involves aggregating and categorizing spend data manually, which limits the level of detail and frequency of the analysis. Traditional methods are effective for broad insights but may fail to uncover granular cost-saving opportunities or identify patterns in real-time.

ML-enabled spend analysis goes a step further by categorizing spend data automatically, identifying trends, and suggesting optimization strategies in real time. Machine learning can analyze spending across different departments, product categories, and regions, revealing hidden opportunities for savings. For example, ML might identify that a certain category has a high variance in pricing across suppliers, suggesting a potential renegotiation for better rates. Or, it could highlight a high level of maverick spending (purchases outside of contracts) and recommend adjustments.

With ML, spend analysis is no longer just a reactive exercise but becomes a proactive process that continually seeks out cost-saving

31

opportunities, aligns spending with budget goals, and provides transparency into procurement spending at a granular level.

5. Risk Management: Reactive vs. Predictive Approaches

Risk management in traditional procurement is typically reactive, with teams addressing risks as they arise based on historical experience and periodic risk assessments. This approach is limited in its ability to anticipate emerging risks, which are often masked by the complexities of global supply chains.

Machine learning changes risk management from a reactive to a predictive function. ML algorithms can analyze multiple risk factors—such as supplier performance trends, geopolitical risks, and environmental factors—and predict potential disruptions before they occur. For instance, an ML system might detect an increased risk of supplier failure based on patterns in late deliveries, quality issues, or even subtle indicators like delayed invoices.

By using ML-driven predictive risk analysis, procurement can take a proactive approach to managing risks, ensuring continuity in the supply chain, and reducing the likelihood of costly disruptions.

6. Contract Analysis and Compliance Monitoring

In traditional procurement, contract analysis and compliance monitoring are often manual processes where procurement teams review contract terms and monitor supplier compliance. This can be time-consuming, and the complexity of contracts may lead to unintentional oversights.

Machine learning enables automated contract analysis, where ML models, particularly those using natural language processing (NLP), can scan, interpret, and analyze contract documents for key clauses, obligations, and compliance requirements. ML-driven systems can flag any deviations from standard terms, identify potential risks embedded in contracts, and automatically monitor compliance milestones. This automation reduces the likelihood of human error, ensures greater compliance, and speeds up the review process, enabling procurement to manage contracts more effectively.

For instance, NLP-powered ML models can analyze contract language and identify potential red flags, such as unfavorable terms or ambiguous clauses. This capability empowers procurement teams to enforce contract compliance more consistently, reducing risks associated with non-compliance and streamlining supplier management.

7. Workforce Skills and Expertise

In traditional procurement, the effectiveness of processes is heavily dependent on the skills, experience, and judgment of procurement professionals. While this expertise is invaluable, it can also limit scalability, as manual work takes time and can be challenging to standardize across teams.

Machine learning allows procurement teams to expand their capabilities without requiring a proportional increase in workforce size. ML-driven systems can perform data analysis, risk assessment, and spend optimization autonomously, allowing procurement professionals to focus on strategic tasks that require human insight and creativity. With ML handling routine analysis, procurement teams can elevate their work to become more strategic partners within the organization, focusing on relationship-building, supplier negotiation, and long-term planning.

Moreover, as procurement professionals gain experience with ML tools, they develop new skills in interpreting ML outputs and using AI insights to guide strategic decisions, enhancing their expertise and value within the organization.

8. Adaptability to Changing Market Conditions

Traditional procurement methods often operate on fixed rules and pre-set workflows, which can make it challenging to adapt to rapid changes in the market or supply chain disruptions. For example, in the event of a sudden market shift, traditional procurement may lack the agility to respond quickly, leading to missed opportunities or delays.

Machine learning offers a significant advantage in adaptability. ML models are designed to learn from new data and adjust their outputs as market conditions evolve. This enables procurement teams to stay agile in the face of change, as ML tools can recalibrate forecasts, identify alternative suppliers, and even recommend changes in sourcing strategies in real time. This adaptability ensures that procurement remains aligned with current market conditions and can respond proactively to shifts in supply and demand.

In conclusion, while traditional procurement methods provide valuable foundations, they are increasingly limited in today's fast-paced and data-rich environment. Machine learning offers a powerful alternative, with capabilities in dynamic data analysis, predictive risk management, automated spend optimization, and adaptability. By integrating ML, procurement teams can unlock new levels of efficiency, resilience, and strategic value, shifting their role from a back-office function to a proactive, data-driven partner in organizational success. This transition positions procurement to thrive in the future, embracing a more agile, data-powered approach to supply chain management.

Chapter 5: Key Benefits of AI and ML in Procurement

The integration of artificial intelligence (AI) and machine learning (ML) into procurement processes is revolutionizing how organizations manage supply chains, suppliers, costs, and compliance. These technologies are driving significant improvements in efficiency, accuracy, and strategic decision-making, providing procurement teams with an unprecedented level of insight and control. As organizations increasingly adopt AI and ML, the benefits become more pronounced, from cost savings to more efficient workflows and enhanced accuracy.

1. Cost Savings

One of the most immediate and impactful benefits of AI and ML in procurement is cost reduction. Traditional procurement processes are often resource-intensive, requiring extensive manual work to analyze spend data, negotiate with suppliers, and manage contracts. AI and ML streamline these activities by automating spend analysis, cost optimization, and supplier negotiations, resulting in significant cost savings.

Spend Analysis and Optimization: ML algorithms analyze procurement data to uncover spending patterns, identify high-cost areas, and suggest cost-saving strategies. For example, an ML model might identify that bulk purchasing or consolidating orders across departments would reduce costs without compromising quality. This analysis, which would be time-consuming to perform manually, is executed rapidly and continuously with ML, enabling procurement teams to adjust their strategies in real time.

Supplier Cost Optimization: AI-powered tools assess supplier pricing, delivery performance, and reliability to help procurement teams negotiate better terms. By analyzing historical transaction data and current market conditions, AI can suggest suppliers offering the best value, contributing to cost savings while maintaining or improving service levels. Procurement teams can also use AI insights to renegotiate contracts with existing suppliers, reducing expenses across categories.

Reducing Maverick Spend: Maverick spending—purchases made outside of established contracts or approved channels—is a common source of unplanned expenses. AI-driven systems can monitor purchase data to detect instances of maverick spend in real-time, allowing procurement teams to intervene and redirect purchases to approved suppliers and channels, helping to reduce unauthorized spending and capture additional savings.

2. Efficiency in Procurement Processes

AI and ML streamline many procurement processes by automating repetitive tasks and minimizing manual intervention. This automation allows procurement professionals to allocate more time to strategic activities, improving overall productivity and efficiency.

Automated Purchase Order (PO) and Invoice Processing: AI-powered systems can automatically generate, process, and approve purchase orders and invoices, reducing the need for human involvement in routine tasks. For example, natural language processing (NLP) algorithms can scan invoices to ensure they match the purchase orders and flag discrepancies for review. This not only reduces processing time but also minimizes errors, enhancing the accuracy of financial records and reducing bottlenecks in the procurement cycle.

Supplier Selection and Management: ML models can analyze supplier data, including delivery times, quality scores, and compliance metrics, to create a supplier scorecard that simplifies the supplier selection process. By automating these evaluations, procurement teams can expedite the selection process, improve supplier performance, and make data-driven decisions on supplier partnerships. Additionally, AI tools can monitor ongoing supplier performance, notifying teams of any performance dips or potential risks in real time.

Demand Forecasting and Inventory Management: AI-driven demand forecasting tools enable procurement teams to predict inventory requirements with greater accuracy. These tools analyze historical data, market trends, and real-time signals to forecast demand, allowing procurement teams to optimize inventory levels and avoid stockouts or excess inventory. Accurate demand forecasting enhances order planning, minimizes rush orders, and leads to cost-effective inventory management.

3. Enhanced Accuracy and Reduced Errors

Manual procurement tasks are prone to human error, especially when managing large volumes of data across multiple suppliers and transactions. AI and ML significantly improve data accuracy by reducing reliance on manual entry and analysis.

Data Validation and Error Reduction: Machine learning algorithms can cross-reference data entries in real-time, identifying discrepancies and correcting errors automatically. For example, AI systems can check if the quantities and prices in an invoice match the corresponding purchase order, flagging any inconsistencies before processing. This level of accuracy helps prevent costly mistakes and ensures data integrity across procurement systems.

Predictive Risk Management: AI enhances the accuracy of risk management by analyzing supplier data and identifying potential risks before they materialize. Machine learning algorithms assess factors such as supplier reliability, economic stability, and geopolitical risks, generating accurate risk predictions. This proactive approach allows procurement teams to address risks before they affect operations, improving overall accuracy in supplier risk assessment.

Compliance Monitoring: AI-powered compliance tools ensure that procurement activities align with regulatory requirements and internal policies. ML models analyze transaction data, identifying any deviations from compliance standards and flagging them for review. This automated monitoring minimizes the chances of compliance errors and helps organizations avoid penalties associated with non-compliance, ensuring that procurement processes remain accurate and aligned with regulations.

4. Strategic Decision-Making and Insights

AI and ML empower procurement teams with real-time insights and predictive analytics, enabling them to make more informed and strategic decisions. These insights transform procurement from a cost-focused function to a strategic partner that drives value and contributes to organizational goals.

Predictive Analytics for Market Trends: Machine learning models analyze vast datasets to identify emerging trends in the market, such as shifts in supplier costs, raw material availability, or changes in demand patterns. These insights allow procurement teams to adjust their strategies in anticipation of market changes, securing better terms or alternative suppliers before costs rise or supply becomes limited.

Supplier Relationship Management (SRM): AI-driven SRM tools analyze supplier performance, contract terms, and transactional data to provide a comprehensive view of each supplier's strengths and weaknesses. This information enables procurement teams to make strategic decisions about supplier partnerships, focusing on suppliers who consistently meet performance benchmarks while addressing issues with those who do not. By leveraging AI insights, procurement teams can build stronger, more strategic supplier relationships, resulting in improved service levels and cost efficiency.

Enhanced Spend Visibility and Control: AI-powered spend analysis tools provide procurement teams with granular insights into spending patterns and trends. These insights help teams identify cost-saving opportunities, optimize budgets, and control spending more effectively. AI also allows procurement teams to perform real-time spend analysis, providing updated insights that guide strategic adjustments and ensure alignment with financial goals.

5. Scalability and Adaptability

As organizations grow and their procurement needs become more complex, AI and ML offer the scalability needed to manage larger volumes of data and transactions without sacrificing accuracy or efficiency.

Automated Workflows for High-Volume Procurement: In large organizations with high transaction volumes, manual processing can quickly become a bottleneck. AI-driven automation scales easily, allowing organizations to handle an increased workload without a proportional increase in labor costs. This scalability enables procurement teams to adapt to business growth without compromising service quality.

Adaptability to Market Changes: Traditional procurement processes are often rigid, relying on set procedures and historical data that may not adapt to rapid market changes. Machine learning, however, allows for continuous learning from new data inputs, making procurement processes more adaptable. For instance, during a supply chain disruption, an AI system can quickly analyze new data to recommend alternative suppliers, sourcing options, or adjustments to inventory levels, helping procurement teams respond proactively to changing conditions.

6. Competitive Advantage

In today's competitive landscape, organizations that adopt AI and ML in procurement gain a strategic advantage over those that rely solely on traditional methods. AI-driven insights and process improvements allow companies to operate more efficiently, reduce costs, and respond to market demands faster than their competitors.

Agility in Procurement Decisions: AI-powered tools enable faster decision-making, allowing procurement teams to seize opportunities quickly. For instance, AI can alert procurement teams to a sudden drop in supplier prices, allowing them to secure lower-cost materials before competitors do. This agility gives organizations a competitive edge by ensuring that procurement operations are responsive to market opportunities.

Innovation and Strategic Growth: By automating routine tasks and providing real-time insights, AI and ML free procurement teams to focus on strategic initiatives and innovation. For example, procurement professionals can explore sustainable sourcing options, develop new supplier partnerships, or implement advanced category management strategies that support long-term growth. These strategic efforts, supported by AI, enable organizations to align procurement with broader business objectives and foster innovation.

In conclusion, the adoption of AI and ML in procurement offers a transformative set of benefits, from cost savings and process efficiency to improved accuracy and strategic agility. By leveraging these technologies, procurement teams can streamline operations, enhance decision-making, and ultimately create more value for their organizations. As procurement becomes increasingly data-driven, AI and ML are not just tools for automation—they are essential components of a forward-thinking, strategically aligned procurement function. This shift positions procurement as a key contributor to organizational success, driving efficiency and innovation in a rapidly evolving market.

Part 2: AI Applications in Procurement

Chapter 6: Supplier Selection and Evaluation with AI

AI plays a pivotal role in supplier selection and evaluation, two foundational activities in procurement. By using AI to analyze vast quantities of data, organizations can gain insights into suppliers' performance, reliability, cost structures, and even alignment with corporate values such as sustainability. Traditional supplier evaluation methods involve time-consuming manual processes and are limited by the amount of data procurement professionals can analyze. AI-driven supplier evaluation, in contrast, introduces speed, accuracy, and the ability to consider a broader range of factors.

1. The Role of AI in Supplier Selection and Evaluation

Supplier selection and evaluation require thorough analysis of several factors, such as quality, price, delivery times, past performance, risk, and compliance with regulations. Traditional procurement methods typically use historical data, industry knowledge, and relationships to make supplier decisions. However, AI provides procurement teams with advanced tools to analyze supplier data more comprehensively and accurately, allowing for more objective and data-driven decisions.

Automating Supplier Discovery: AI algorithms can analyze a company's specific requirements, such as product specifications, delivery timelines, and budget constraints, to identify suppliers that meet these criteria. Rather than searching through databases or relying on word-of-mouth recommendations, procurement teams can use AI to quickly and accurately discover potential suppliers from large datasets, industry reports, and even open-source information.

Data-Driven Evaluation: Traditional evaluations may rely on subjective metrics, but AI allows procurement teams to use concrete, data-driven criteria to compare suppliers. For example, an AI system might analyze product quality metrics, warranty claims, and customer reviews to give procurement professionals a complete picture of each supplier's performance history, enhancing the reliability of the selection process.

2. Criteria for Supplier Evaluation Using AI

AI can enhance supplier evaluation by assessing multiple dimensions of supplier performance. These factors range from quantitative metrics, such as cost and delivery times, to qualitative aspects like supplier reputation and alignment with corporate social responsibility (CSR) values.

45

Cost and Quality: AI analyzes price trends and cost structures across suppliers, evaluating how pricing aligns with quality benchmarks. By tracking cost fluctuations over time, AI can identify suppliers that offer the best value for money. Moreover, quality metrics can be assessed through AI-based analyses of product defect rates, complaint records, and warranty claims, enabling procurement to focus on cost-efficient suppliers without sacrificing quality.

Delivery and Reliability: Machine learning models can analyze historical delivery data to evaluate supplier reliability. This includes assessing average delivery times, on-time delivery percentages, and delays across previous orders. If a supplier consistently meets deadlines and demonstrates promptness, it is flagged as a reliable option. Alternatively, if AI identifies patterns of delay or issues with specific regions or seasons, procurement can make more informed decisions on delivery performance.

Risk and Compliance: AI can cross-reference supplier data with external databases to identify any risk factors, such as financial instability, political risk, or compliance violations. For example, AI can monitor news sources, legal records, and financial reports to assess a supplier's stability. This insight helps procurement teams avoid suppliers with a history of non-compliance or financial instability, reducing risk exposure.

Sustainability and CSR Alignment: AI tools that perform sentiment analysis and natural language processing (NLP) can assess supplier practices regarding sustainability and social responsibility. By analyzing public records, supplier declarations, and sustainability reports, AI provides insights into whether suppliers adhere to environmental standards or CSR values. Companies aiming for sustainable procurement can use this information to choose suppliers whose values align with their own.

3. Benefits of AI-Driven Supplier Selection

Leveraging AI in supplier selection offers significant advantages, especially in terms of accuracy, efficiency, and strategic alignment. Key benefits include:

Enhanced Objectivity: AI brings objectivity to supplier evaluation, reducing the impact of personal biases or preconceived notions. Machine learning models evaluate suppliers based on quantifiable data, leading to fairer assessments and enabling procurement teams to make more consistent choices across departments or geographies.

Real-Time Evaluation and Responsiveness: One of AI's unique capabilities is real-time data processing, enabling procurement teams to make quicker decisions. When urgent needs arise, such as during supply chain disruptions, AI can swiftly evaluate available suppliers, making it possible to pivot to alternative sources without delay.

Predictive Insights: By identifying emerging trends and risks, AI allows procurement teams to act proactively. For instance, if AI detects an increase in material costs from a particular supplier, procurement can anticipate cost escalations and either negotiate or find alternative suppliers. This predictive capability is particularly valuable in volatile markets, where shifts in supplier performance or costs can significantly impact operations.

4. The AI-Powered Supplier Selection Process

An AI-driven supplier selection process typically follows these steps:

Requirement Identification: The procurement team inputs key requirements, such as cost limits, quality standards, delivery windows, and specific certifications or compliance needs.

Supplier Identification: AI algorithms search databases and open-source information to identify a pool of potential suppliers that match the set criteria.

Data Collection: AI gathers data from various sources, including financial reports, regulatory databases, news articles, and internal performance data, to build comprehensive profiles for each supplier.

Supplier Scoring and Ranking: The AI system uses a scoring model to rank suppliers based on relevant metrics, such as cost, delivery, quality, and risk.

Recommendation Generation: The AI system provides a list of top-ranked suppliers with a breakdown of each supplier's strengths and weaknesses, allowing procurement to make an informed choice based on objective data.

5. Tools and Technologies Used in AI-Powered Supplier Selection

Various AI-powered tools and technologies are now available to assist procurement teams in supplier selection and evaluation. Some of these include:

Natural Language Processing (NLP): NLP enables the analysis of unstructured text data, such as supplier reviews, public statements, and industry reports. For instance, NLP can scan supplier websites for keywords related to sustainability, quality, or ethics, helping procurement teams evaluate alignment with company values.

Machine Learning Algorithms: Machine learning models process historical performance data to predict future supplier performance. These algorithms evaluate numerous factors, including price fluctuations, defect rates, and delivery consistency, to anticipate how well a supplier will perform over time.

Sentiment Analysis: Sentiment analysis algorithms assess public opinion and reviews about a supplier. By examining social media, customer feedback, and news mentions, procurement teams gain insights into the supplier's reputation, potentially flagging risks that aren't evident in standard performance data.

Robotic Process Automation (RPA): RPA streamlines repetitive tasks, such as document management and initial supplier data entry, allowing procurement professionals to focus on more complex evaluations. RPA also assists with automated scoring and ranking of suppliers based on AI-generated data.

6. Case Studies of AI in Supplier Selection

Several companies have successfully implemented AI for supplier selection, realizing substantial improvements in procurement efficiency and accuracy.

Case Study 1: Reducing Costs with Automated Supplier Selection

A global electronics manufacturer adopted an AI-powered supplier selection tool to manage hundreds of suppliers. By automating spend analysis and evaluating cost versus performance data across suppliers, the company reduced its sourcing costs by 20% and shortened its supplier selection time by 30%. This approach allowed the company to respond quickly to market changes, adapting its supply base to meet evolving demands.

Case Study 2: Improving Supplier Compliance in Healthcare Procurement

A healthcare procurement organization implemented AI to improve compliance in supplier selection. The AI system monitored each supplier's adherence to regulatory standards, performing automated checks on financial stability and risk factors. By using AI, the organization reduced supplier compliance issues by 15% and avoided costly disruptions due to non-compliance.

7. Challenges and Considerations in AI-Driven Supplier Selection

Despite its advantages, using AI for supplier selection has some challenges that procurement teams need to consider:

Data Quality and Availability: AI models rely on high-quality, relevant data. If supplier data is incomplete or inconsistent, AI may not produce accurate results. Ensuring data quality and working with reliable data sources is critical to successful AI implementation.

Bias and Fairness in Algorithms: AI models can inadvertently introduce biases if they are trained on biased data. Procurement teams should continuously evaluate and refine their AI models to avoid reinforcing biases in supplier evaluations.

Integration with Existing Systems: Implementing AI in procurement may require integration with existing procurement and ERP systems.

Ensuring seamless data flow between these systems can pose technical challenges that may need IT support and dedicated resources.

In conclusion, AI is revolutionizing supplier selection and evaluation by enhancing objectivity, efficiency, and data-driven decision-making. AI-powered supplier evaluation allows procurement teams to assess suppliers based on diverse criteria, including cost, quality, delivery reliability, and compliance, leading to more strategic partnerships and improved supplier relationships. By implementing AI in supplier selection, organizations gain a competitive edge in supply chain agility, risk management, and sustainability, positioning procurement as a strategic enabler of organizational goals.

Chapter 7: AI-Driven Demand Forecasting

Demand forecasting is a vital component of procurement and supply chain management, helping organizations predict future demand for products and services accurately. Traditionally, demand forecasting has relied on historical sales data, market trends, and judgment-based predictions. However, these conventional methods often lack precision, particularly in dynamic markets. AI-driven demand forecasting, specifically using machine learning (ML), revolutionizes this process by bringing predictive accuracy, real-time responsiveness, and advanced pattern recognition to the forefront of procurement strategies.

1. Understanding AI-Driven Demand Forecasting

AI-driven demand forecasting uses machine learning models to analyze historical data, identify trends, and predict future demand patterns. By processing complex datasets, such as sales figures, seasonal variations, customer behavior, and economic indicators, ML algorithms enable procurement teams to anticipate demand shifts accurately and plan accordingly. These models are designed to continuously learn and adapt to changing market conditions, enhancing their forecasting accuracy over time.

Machine learning algorithms use supervised and unsupervised learning methods to make predictions:

Supervised Learning: In this approach, ML algorithms are trained on labeled data (where the outcome is known) to forecast future demand based on similar patterns. For instance, supervised learning can identify how past promotions or events influenced sales, helping to predict the effects of future promotions.

Unsupervised Learning: Unsupervised learning helps to discover hidden patterns in demand data. It identifies customer purchasing behaviors, such as cyclical trends or seasonality, without pre-existing labels, which can be especially helpful in uncovering previously unrecognized patterns.

2. Benefits of AI-Driven Demand Forecasting

AI-based demand forecasting offers significant advantages over traditional forecasting methods, including increased accuracy, efficiency, and strategic responsiveness. Some of the primary benefits include:

Higher Accuracy: Machine learning models analyze vast amounts of data and detect intricate patterns often missed by traditional methods.

53

This improved accuracy helps procurement professionals reduce forecasting errors, which translates to better inventory management and cost savings.

Adaptability to Dynamic Markets: Unlike traditional models, which may require frequent manual updates, ML algorithms automatically adjust to new data, making them well-suited for volatile or unpredictable markets. Real-time adaptability enables businesses to respond faster to sudden demand changes.

Reduced Stockouts and Overstocks: Accurate forecasting minimizes the risk of stockouts (shortages) and overstocks (excess inventory), both of which have costly implications. By predicting demand more precisely, companies can optimize inventory levels to better match actual sales, reducing warehousing costs and improving cash flow.

Enhanced Customer Satisfaction: Accurate forecasting allows businesses to meet customer demand promptly. With optimal stock levels and reduced lead times, companies can improve service levels, ensuring product availability without excessive delays.

3. How AI Models Enhance Demand Forecasting Accuracy

Machine learning models bring several technical enhancements to the demand forecasting process, including:

Pattern Recognition in Complex Datasets: AI-driven models are adept at identifying patterns in large datasets. For example, a retail company might use ML to analyze historical sales data alongside external factors like weather patterns, economic indicators, and competitor actions to predict demand surges or dips.

Seasonal and Cyclical Trend Analysis: Machine learning algorithms can recognize seasonal trends and adjust forecasts accordingly. A machine learning model may, for example, detect that demand for certain products surges during specific seasons or after paydays, allowing businesses to adjust inventory to match these cyclical trends.

Predictive Analysis Based on External Factors: In addition to internal data, machine learning models incorporate external variables—such as economic conditions, social trends, and even local events—that can impact demand. For instance, an ML model may predict increased demand for rain gear during a season of unusually high rainfall by analyzing weather forecasts and historical data.

Handling Anomalies and Outliers: Demand data can include unexpected spikes or drops caused by one-off events or anomalies. AI-based models recognize these outliers and adjust forecasts accordingly, reducing the likelihood of overreactions to short-term anomalies.

4. Key Machine Learning Models for Demand Forecasting

There are several types of machine learning models commonly used in AI-driven demand forecasting, each with unique strengths:

Time Series Analysis (ARIMA, SARIMA): Time series models like ARIMA (AutoRegressive Integrated Moving Average) and SARIMA (Seasonal ARIMA) are popular for demand forecasting as they account for seasonality and time-based trends. These models are particularly useful in stable markets where demand fluctuates predictably.

Recurrent Neural Networks (RNNs) and Long Short-Term Memory (LSTM): RNNs and LSTMs are deep learning models designed for sequence data, making them ideal for time-dependent tasks like demand forecasting. They analyze the sequence of past demand and other time-based factors to predict future trends, excelling in complex environments with volatile demand patterns.

Gradient Boosting Machines (GBMs) and Random Forests: These ensemble models are well-suited for cases where demand depends on a wide array of external and internal factors. They offer high predictive accuracy by combining multiple weak predictors to create a robust model.

Prophet: Developed by Facebook, Prophet is a forecasting model that handles seasonality, holidays, and other time-based trends well. It's commonly used in demand forecasting as it's user-friendly and yields accurate results with relatively little data processing.

5. AI Demand Forecasting in Action: Real-World Applications

AI-driven demand forecasting is widely adopted across industries, with notable improvements in inventory control, production planning, and customer satisfaction. Here are a few examples of AI-driven demand forecasting in action:

Retail Industry: Retailers often face fluctuating demand based on promotions, holidays, and seasonality. With AI, they can analyze past sales data, customer behavior, and social media trends to forecast demand accurately. For example, a fashion retailer could predict which clothing items will be in high demand during specific seasons, ensuring they have sufficient stock without over-purchasing.

Manufacturing Sector: Manufacturers use AI-driven demand forecasting to optimize production schedules and resource allocation. By predicting demand for finished goods, manufacturers can adjust production levels, optimize workforce scheduling, and reduce excess inventory.

Food and Beverage Industry: Companies in this sector deal with perishable products, making accurate demand forecasting crucial. AI-based models allow food and beverage companies to forecast demand precisely, minimizing waste while ensuring products are fresh and available.

6. Implementing AI-Driven Demand Forecasting: Challenges and Considerations

Despite the benefits, implementing AI-driven demand forecasting is not without its challenges. Companies need to address specific considerations to ensure effective deployment:

Data Quality and Availability: Accurate AI models depend on high-quality, relevant data. If data is inaccurate, incomplete, or outdated, forecasting models may produce unreliable predictions. Businesses must invest in data cleaning and integration processes to ensure a robust data pipeline.

Model Selection and Complexity: Choosing the right model is crucial for effective forecasting. Some models may require extensive computational resources and expertise, so companies must balance accuracy with practical considerations like cost and ease of use.

Integration with Existing Systems: AI-driven forecasting tools should integrate seamlessly with other supply chain and procurement systems, such as Enterprise Resource Planning (ERP) or Warehouse Management Systems (WMS). Integration enables real-time data flow and facilitates a smooth transition from forecasting to actionable planning.

Change Management and Skills Development: AI-driven forecasting often requires a shift in organizational mindset and skill sets. Procurement and supply chain teams must receive training on new technologies and analytical methods to leverage AI capabilities fully.

AI-driven demand forecasting has transformed how companies predict and respond to market demands. With machine learning models, businesses can achieve unprecedented levels of forecasting accuracy, enabling them to optimize inventory levels, reduce costs, and improve customer satisfaction. As industries continue to navigate dynamic markets, AI-based demand forecasting will become increasingly essential, empowering procurement teams to make proactive, data-driven decisions.

By integrating AI into demand forecasting, organizations not only stay competitive but also establish a foundation for smarter, more agile supply chains that can adapt to changes quickly and efficiently.

Chapter 8: Spend Analytics and Cost Optimization

Spend analytics plays a critical role in procurement and financial planning, helping businesses understand where their money is going, identify cost-saving opportunities, and improve budgeting accuracy. Traditional spend analysis has often relied on manual data analysis and simple reporting tools, which limit the depth and accuracy of insights that organizations can extract. AI-powered spend analytics, however, enables procurement teams to analyze large, complex datasets automatically, delivering real-time insights and uncovering hidden patterns in spending data that might go unnoticed with traditional methods.

Leveraging artificial intelligence for spend analytics and cost optimization allows procurement professionals to make informed, data-driven decisions that ultimately reduce expenses and improve financial performance. This chapter explores the fundamentals of AI in spend analytics, its benefits, and practical applications for cost optimization.

1. Understanding Spend Analytics in Procurement

Spend analytics refers to the process of collecting, cleaning, categorizing, and analyzing spend data to improve visibility into how an organization's money is spent. This process provides a detailed overview of all expenditures, broken down by categories such as suppliers, departments, product types, and regions.

Traditionally, spend analytics has been a time-consuming process requiring extensive manual work to clean and organize data from multiple sources, such as invoices, purchase orders, and financial reports. AI, however, can automate much of this data cleansing and categorization process, making it easier to generate accurate, actionable insights with minimal manual effort.

With AI-driven spend analytics, procurement professionals can:

Identify and analyze spending patterns.

Categorize spend into relevant segments.

Discover opportunities for cost-saving and supplier negotiation.

Monitor compliance with budgeting and procurement policies.

2. How AI Enhances Spend Analytics

AI enhances spend analytics by applying advanced machine learning algorithms, natural language processing (NLP), and data automation techniques to manage and interpret large volumes of unstructured data from diverse sources. Here are some ways AI revolutionizes spend analytics:

Automated Data Cleansing and Classification: AI algorithms can clean and standardize data automatically, removing duplicates, correcting errors, and categorizing transactions accurately. By leveraging machine learning, AI systems "learn" the specific spending categories and behaviors of a business, enabling precise classification across complex datasets.NLP for Enhanced Data Analysis: Natural language processing enables AI to analyze unstructured text in procurement documents, such as contract terms, invoices, and email communications with suppliers. NLP helps to extract and interpret key data points from these sources, contributing to a more comprehensive spend analysis.

Pattern Recognition and Trend Analysis: Machine learning models excel at identifying patterns in spending behavior, such as seasonal purchasing trends, repetitive expenses, and areas of overspending. By recognizing these patterns, procurement teams can anticipate upcoming expenses more accurately and identify opportunities for optimization.

Anomaly Detection: AI-powered spend analytics can detect unusual or unexpected spending patterns that might indicate compliance issues, waste, or even fraud. By flagging these anomalies, procurement teams can take corrective actions quickly, avoiding unnecessary expenses and ensuring adherence to spending policies.

3. Key Benefits of AI-Driven Spend Analytics

Implementing AI in spend analytics delivers multiple benefits, transforming the way organizations manage their expenditures and pursue cost-saving opportunities. Some of the key advantages include:

Improved Budgeting Accuracy: With deeper insights into past spending behavior, procurement teams can set more realistic budgets and anticipate costs with greater precision. By understanding where money has been spent historically, they can align budgets with actual needs and avoid over- or under-budgeting.

Strategic Sourcing and Supplier Negotiation: AI-driven spend analysis enables procurement teams to assess supplier performance, compare pricing structures, and evaluate vendor-related spending patterns. Armed with these insights, teams are better equipped to negotiate favorable terms, consolidate suppliers, and pursue strategic sourcing opportunities that lower overall costs.

Increased Cost Savings: By identifying areas of overspending or waste, AI-powered analytics helps organizations implement cost-cutting measures more effectively. This may include switching suppliers, renegotiating contracts, or optimizing inventory levels based on historical usage patterns.

Enhanced Compliance and Risk Mitigation: AI can monitor and enforce compliance with procurement policies, flagging transactions that deviate from approved budgets or supplier agreements. This ensures adherence to company policies, reduces regulatory risk, and minimizes unnecessary spending.

4. AI-Powered Spend Analytics Tools and Techniques

There are several AI-powered tools and techniques that organizations can use to enhance spend analytics. Here are some commonly adopted methods:

Spend Classification Models: Machine learning models can classify spend data based on predefined or learned categories, such as supplier types, departments, or regions. These models help procurement teams segment their spending, making it easier to analyze and manage each category effectively.

Predictive Analytics for Future Spend: Predictive analytics use historical data to forecast future spending patterns, allowing companies to plan and budget more accurately. This capability is especially valuable in industries with cyclical or seasonal spending patterns, enabling proactive cost management.

Supplier Performance and Spend Visibility Dashboards: AI-powered dashboards visualize spending data, providing procurement teams with a real-time view of where money is being spent, who the key suppliers are, and how costs are trending over time. These dashboards support data-driven decision-making and allow users to filter data by various categories, such as supplier, product, and region.

Dynamic Reporting and Real-Time Insights: Traditional reporting methods are often static, providing only a snapshot of past spending. AI-driven analytics tools, however, offer dynamic reporting that can be updated in real-time as new data becomes available. This allows procurement teams to respond quickly to spending changes and adjust budgets accordingly.

5. Real-World Applications of AI in Spend Analytics and Cost Optimization

AI-driven spend analytics has become an integral part of procurement in industries ranging from manufacturing to retail and healthcare. Here are some examples of how organizations use AI to optimize costs:

Retail Sector: In retail, AI-powered spend analytics allows companies to track expenditures on inventory, marketing, and logistics in real-time. By analyzing spending data, retailers can identify trends and reduce excess spending, such as optimizing seasonal purchasing and minimizing waste in supply chain processes.

Manufacturing: Manufacturers use AI-driven analytics to monitor spending on raw materials, production equipment, and energy costs. By analyzing spending trends, manufacturers can negotiate better rates with suppliers, control expenses, and implement cost-cutting measures based on accurate forecasts of material needs.

Healthcare: The healthcare sector faces high procurement costs for medical supplies, pharmaceuticals, and equipment. AI-powered spend analytics helps healthcare providers track spending, improve budget allocation, and reduce costs through strategic sourcing and supplier negotiation.

6. Steps for Implementing AI-Driven Spend Analytics

Implementing AI-driven spend analytics involves a structured approach to ensure data quality, model selection, and integration with existing systems. Here are the steps to achieve effective AI-powered spend analysis:

Data Collection and Preparation: The first step is gathering relevant spend data from various sources, including invoices, purchase orders, contracts, and financial records. This data should be standardized and cleansed to ensure accuracy before feeding it into AI models.

Model Selection and Training: Choose machine learning models based on the specific needs and complexity of your spend analysis. Common models include classification algorithms, decision trees, and neural networks. Training these models with historical data allows them to identify patterns and trends in spending behavior.

Integration with Procurement Systems: AI-driven spend analytics tools should be integrated with the organization's existing procurement software, such as ERP or supplier management systems. This ensures a seamless flow of data and real-time visibility into spending activities.

Visualization and Reporting Tools: Implement visualization tools, like dashboards, to present insights from spend analytics in a clear, user-friendly format. This helps procurement teams understand spending trends quickly and make informed decisions.

Ongoing Model Evaluation and Refinement: AI models must be monitored regularly to ensure accuracy and relevance. By refining these models and updating them with new data, organizations can maintain a high level of accuracy in spend forecasting and cost optimization.

7. Challenges and Considerations in AI-Driven Spend Analytics

While AI-driven spend analytics provides numerous benefits, there are challenges that organizations must address:

Data Privacy and Compliance: Organizations must ensure that spend data is handled in compliance with data privacy regulations, especially when dealing with sensitive financial information. Robust data governance policies are essential to protect against unauthorized access.

Data Quality and Consistency: AI models are only as effective as the data they process. Inaccurate, incomplete, or inconsistent data can lead to misleading insights. Procurement teams need to invest in data quality initiatives to ensure reliable outcomes from AI-driven analytics.

Change Management: Shifting from traditional spend analysis to AI-driven analytics requires a change in mindset and skills. Procurement teams need training on new tools, analytics methods, and data interpretation to fully leverage AI capabilities.

AI-driven spend analytics is a powerful tool that empowers organizations to gain deeper insights into spending patterns, optimize costs, and make smarter budgeting decisions. By automating data processing and enhancing visibility into procurement expenditures, AI transforms spend analysis from a manual, time-consuming task into a proactive, strategic function. As companies continue to navigate competitive markets, the adoption of AI in spend analytics will become increasingly critical, enabling organizations to stay agile, maximize cost savings, and strengthen their financial performance.

Chapter 9: Category Management with Machine Learning

Category management is a strategic approach to procurement that organizes purchases into categories with similar goods or services, making it easier to manage supplier relationships, track expenditures, and optimize procurement strategies. Machine learning (ML) adds a new dimension to category management by enabling data-driven insights that help procurement teams make smarter, more efficient decisions about sourcing and category strategies. By applying ML techniques, organizations can better understand demand patterns, optimize pricing, and align category strategies with overall business goals.

This chapter covers the fundamentals of category management, the role of machine learning in enhancing its effectiveness, and practical applications for leveraging ML in category strategy development.

1. What Is Category Management?

Category management is a procurement strategy where products or services with similar characteristics are grouped into distinct categories, such as office supplies, raw materials, or IT services. Managing these categories collectively enables organizations to make bulk purchases, secure volume discounts, and streamline supplier management. A well-organized category strategy can significantly reduce costs, improve supplier relationships, and align purchasing decisions with the organization's overall goals.

The main objectives of category management are to:

Improve cost-effectiveness by consolidating purchases.

Ensure a consistent supply of goods and services.

Enhance supplier performance and mitigate supply chain risks.

Foster strategic supplier partnerships for long-term benefits.

Traditional category management relies on historical data and manual analysis, which can be time-consuming and limits the scope of insights that procurement teams can extract. Machine learning, however, allows for automated analysis, predictive modeling, and deeper insights into spending behavior and supplier performance.

2. How Machine Learning Enhances Category Management

Machine learning brings several advantages to category management, enabling procurement teams to work more proactively and strategically. Key ways ML enhances category management include:

Automated Data Categorization and Classification: Machine learning algorithms can automatically categorize purchasing data, analyzing spending records to sort products and services into predefined categories. This capability reduces the manual work required to manage categories and allows for more precise classification of complex data sets.

Predictive Demand Forecasting: By analyzing historical data and external market trends, ML models can predict future demand within each category. Predictive analytics help procurement teams anticipate fluctuations in demand, adjust inventory levels, and plan purchasing activities in advance, preventing shortages or overstocking.

Dynamic Pricing Analysis: ML can analyze pricing trends over time and across various suppliers, identifying patterns that affect category costs. Procurement teams can use these insights to negotiate better prices, determine the best times to buy, or switch to suppliers with more favorable pricing structures.

Supplier Performance Insights: By analyzing supplier data within each category, machine learning can reveal valuable insights into supplier performance, reliability, and risk factors. This enables procurement teams to make data-driven decisions when choosing suppliers and maintaining strategic supplier relationships.

Cost Optimization and Savings Identification: ML identifies opportunities for cost reduction by finding efficiencies within each category. This might include consolidating suppliers, reducing redundancies, or switching to lower-cost alternatives without sacrificing quality.

3. Key Benefits of ML-Driven Category Management

Machine learning offers several compelling benefits for category management in procurement:

Improved Efficiency and Reduced Costs: ML automates the time-consuming tasks of data classification, trend analysis, and spend optimization, freeing up procurement teams to focus on strategic activities. This leads to more efficient processes and reduced operational costs.

Enhanced Decision-Making with Data-Driven Insights: With ML, category managers have access to real-time data insights that improve their decision-making capabilities. These insights enable teams to make well-informed choices on supplier selection, pricing strategies, and inventory management.

Better Supplier Relationships: ML insights into supplier performance allow procurement teams to proactively address issues, negotiate more effectively, and foster better partnerships. This contributes to stronger relationships with key suppliers and ensures a more resilient supply chain.

Risk Mitigation: ML models can identify risks within each category, such as potential supply chain disruptions, price volatility, or supplier performance issues. By flagging these risks, category managers can take preemptive measures to minimize the impact on operations.

4. Practical Applications of Machine Learning in Category Management

Below are some practical applications of ML in enhancing category management:

Spend Analysis and Categorization: ML can automatically categorize procurement data based on attributes such as item type, supplier, and cost. For instance, natural language processing (NLP) techniques can analyze the descriptions of purchase orders and invoices to assign items to the correct categories. This not only speeds up the process but also ensures greater accuracy in spend analysis.

Demand Forecasting for Category-Level Inventory Planning: Demand forecasting models, such as time-series analysis, help procurement teams anticipate future needs within each category. This capability allows for more precise inventory planning, minimizing waste and optimizing stock levels based on predicted demand patterns.

Pricing and Cost Prediction Models: ML algorithms can analyze historical pricing trends to predict future cost fluctuations within each category. For example, regression analysis models may highlight seasonal pricing trends for raw materials, helping category managers make informed purchasing decisions when prices are most favorable.

Supplier Segmentation and Evaluation: ML helps categorize suppliers based on factors like cost-effectiveness, reliability, quality, and delivery performance. By clustering suppliers based on these attributes, procurement teams can prioritize those with higher strategic value and make better sourcing decisions aligned with category objectives.

Continuous Monitoring of Category Performance: ML-based systems can provide real-time insights into each category's performance, offering continuous feedback on spending trends, cost efficiency, and supplier compliance. This allows category managers to make adjustments as needed to optimize category strategies over time.

5. Steps for Implementing Machine Learning in Category Management

Implementing machine learning in category management requires a strategic approach. Here are the steps to follow:

Data Collection and Preparation: Start by gathering relevant data, such as spend data, supplier information, and historical demand records. Ensure that the data is cleaned, standardized, and structured to allow for effective analysis by ML models.

Define Category Objectives: Clarify the specific objectives for each category, such as cost reduction, risk mitigation, or supplier consolidation. These objectives will guide the selection of ML models and analytics techniques.

Select and Train ML Models: Based on the category goals, select appropriate ML models, such as classification algorithms for data categorization, regression models for pricing analysis, or clustering models for supplier segmentation. Train the models with historical data to develop accurate and actionable insights.

Integrate with Procurement Systems: To ensure seamless data flow, integrate ML tools with existing procurement systems, such as ERP software or spend management platforms. This integration enables real-time data updates and continuous category performance monitoring.

Implement Dashboards and Reporting Tools: Visualization tools like dashboards can help category managers view insights generated by ML models in an easy-to-understand format. These tools support faster decision-making by presenting real-time data on category performance.

Monitor and Refine Models: ML models should be continuously evaluated and refined to maintain accuracy. Regularly updating models with new data helps keep insights relevant and reliable, allowing for ongoing optimization of category strategies.

6. Challenges and Considerations in ML-Driven Category Management

While ML-driven category management offers significant advantages, there are several challenges and considerations that organizations should keep in mind:

Data Quality and Consistency: The accuracy of ML models depends on high-quality data. Procurement teams must invest in data cleansing and standardization processes to avoid misleading insights and ensure the reliability of category management models.

Complexity in Model Selection: Selecting the right ML models requires technical expertise, as different algorithms are suited to specific tasks. Organizations may need to partner with data science professionals or invest in training to develop the necessary skills.

Change Management and Training: Introducing ML into category management requires a shift in traditional processes and mindsets. Procurement teams need to be trained on new tools and analytics methods, fostering a data-driven culture within the organization.

Cost of Implementation: Implementing ML solutions can be costly, particularly for organizations with limited budgets. However, the long-term cost savings and efficiency gains typically offset initial implementation expenses.

7. Real-World Examples of ML in Category Management

Many organizations across various industries have successfully implemented ML to improve category management. Here are a few real-world examples:

Retail Industry: Retailers use ML to categorize products and optimize category-based procurement decisions. ML insights enable them to track seasonal demand patterns, adjust inventory levels, and manage supplier relationships effectively.

Manufacturing Sector: Manufacturers leverage ML to predict raw material costs and anticipate fluctuations in demand for critical supplies. These predictions help them negotiate more favorable contracts with suppliers and maintain an optimal stock level for each category.

Healthcare Providers: Healthcare organizations use ML for supplier segmentation and performance evaluation, helping them secure cost-effective supplies of medical equipment and pharmaceuticals. ML-powered category management has allowed healthcare providers to reduce procurement costs and ensure supply continuity.

Machine learning is transforming category management by providing procurement teams with accurate, data-driven insights that enhance decision-making, reduce costs, and improve supplier relationships. By leveraging ML techniques, organizations can automate the classification and analysis of category data, forecast demand with greater accuracy, and optimize pricing and supplier strategies. As organizations continue to embrace digital transformation, ML-driven category management will play a pivotal role in helping procurement teams meet their strategic objectives, ultimately contributing to the organization's success in a competitive market.

Chapter 10: Smart Contracting and Contract Management

In procurement, effective contract management is essential for ensuring supplier performance, risk management, and regulatory compliance. With the evolution of artificial intelligence (AI) and automation, smart contracting has become a transformative approach to contract management, enhancing both efficiency and accuracy. AI-driven contract management solutions can help procurement teams analyze contract terms, mitigate risks, and ensure compliance with legal and regulatory standards.

This chapter discusses the concept of smart contracting, the role of AI in contract analysis, key applications in risk mitigation and compliance, and the practical benefits of AI in optimizing contract management processes.

1. The Basics of Contract Management in Procurement

Contract management involves creating, reviewing, executing, and monitoring contracts to ensure both parties fulfill their agreed-upon obligations. For procurement teams, contract management is central to securing favorable terms, minimizing risks, and protecting the organization from supply chain disruptions and compliance issues. Effective contract management enables procurement teams to:

Secure competitive pricing and favorable terms with suppliers.

Establish clear obligations and expectations for suppliers.

Identify and mitigate potential risks.

Ensure adherence to legal and regulatory standards.

Monitor supplier performance against contract requirements.

Traditional contract management relies heavily on manual processes, requiring teams to review and analyze large amounts of contract data. This can be labor-intensive, time-consuming, and prone to human error. However, AI-driven smart contracting offers a way to automate these tasks, improving efficiency and ensuring accuracy in managing procurement contracts.

2. What Is Smart Contracting?

Smart contracting refers to using AI and automation to streamline and optimize contract management processes. By leveraging AI, procurement teams can automatically analyze contract documents, extract relevant information, and identify critical terms or compliance issues. Smart contracting tools use natural language processing (NLP) and machine learning algorithms to understand contract language, helping teams make better, faster decisions.

Some common features of smart contracting include:

Automated Contract Analysis: AI-driven tools can read and analyze contracts, extracting critical information such as payment terms, delivery schedules, and termination clauses. This reduces manual review time and highlights essential contract details.

Risk Assessment and Mitigation: AI can evaluate contracts for potential risks, such as unfavorable terms or non-compliance with legal requirements. It can also flag clauses that may expose the organization to financial or operational risks.

Compliance Monitoring: AI tools can automatically track contracts for compliance with regulatory standards, alerting procurement teams to potential issues before they become costly problems.

Lifecycle Management: Smart contracting platforms enable end-to-end contract lifecycle management, from drafting and negotiation to performance tracking and renewal. By automating the contract lifecycle, organizations can ensure timely renewals, amendments, and terminations.

3. Key Applications of AI in Contract Management

AI plays a transformative role in contract management by automating analysis, identifying risks, and ensuring compliance. Below are some of the primary applications of AI in smart contracting:

Contract Review and Analysis: NLP algorithms in AI tools can read and interpret contract language, extracting relevant information and presenting it in a user-friendly format. This allows procurement teams to quickly understand key terms, payment schedules, penalties, and other contract details without having to manually read through each document.

Risk Identification and Mitigation: AI-driven tools can evaluate contracts for potential risks, such as high penalty clauses, restrictive exclusivity terms, or lack of termination options. By identifying these risks early, procurement teams can take steps to renegotiate terms or implement safeguards.

Automated Compliance Checks: Regulatory and industry standards often require specific terms or clauses in contracts. AI can scan contracts for these requirements, ensuring compliance and alerting teams to any missing or non-compliant language. This is particularly useful for organizations operating in regulated industries, where non-compliance can lead to significant penalties.

Smart Contracting with Blockchain Integration: Although separate from AI, blockchain technology is often associated with smart contracts, which are self-executing contracts that automatically enforce the terms written within them. Combining AI with blockchain can provide a powerful solution for contract management, allowing for automated performance tracking and real-time compliance verification.

4. Benefits of AI-Driven Smart Contracting in Procurement

Integrating AI into contract management offers numerous benefits, allowing procurement teams to operate more strategically, reduce risks, and increase efficiency. Some of the key benefits include:

Enhanced Efficiency: AI-powered contract analysis is much faster than manual review, allowing procurement teams to manage a larger volume of contracts in less time. This efficiency helps reduce the backlog of contract reviews, especially during peak contracting periods.

Improved Accuracy and Consistency: AI reduces the risk of human error by automatically analyzing contract data and ensuring consistency across multiple contracts. This can be especially valuable for organizations with complex supplier networks and diverse procurement needs.

Proactive Risk Management: AI's ability to detect potential risks in contract terms enables procurement teams to act proactively. By identifying issues early, teams can address potential problems before they lead to financial or operational disruptions.

Better Compliance Assurance: Compliance with legal and regulatory standards is critical in contract management. AI-driven compliance monitoring ensures that contracts adhere to necessary regulations, reducing the risk of penalties or legal liabilities.

Data-Driven Decision-Making: By analyzing historical contract data, AI can provide insights into supplier performance, contract trends, and potential areas for cost savings. These insights enable procurement teams to make data-driven decisions about future contracts and supplier relationships.

5. Implementing AI-Driven Contract Management in Procurement

To successfully integrate AI into contract management, organizations should follow these steps:

Assess Current Contract Management Practices: Review existing contract management processes to identify areas where AI could improve efficiency, reduce risk, or enhance compliance. This assessment helps determine which AI tools and features are most relevant to the organization's needs.

Choose the Right AI-Powered Contract Management Solution: Many contract management platforms now offer AI capabilities. Selecting the right tool depends on the organization's requirements, including the volume of contracts, industry regulations, and budget constraints.

Prepare and Standardize Contract Data: AI-driven contract management relies on high-quality data, so it's essential to standardize contract language and format where possible. This allows AI algorithms to interpret and analyze contract data accurately.

Integrate with Existing Procurement Systems: For seamless data flow, integrate AI-driven contract management tools with procurement and ERP systems. This enables real-time data updates and allows procurement teams to access all contract-related information in one place.

Train Procurement Teams: Teams should receive training on how to use AI-driven contract management tools effectively. This may involve learning new skills in data interpretation, risk analysis, and compliance monitoring.

Monitor and Optimize: Continuous monitoring and optimization ensure that AI tools continue to deliver value. Regularly updating the AI algorithms with new contract data and refining processes based on feedback can improve results over time.

6. Challenges and Considerations in AI-Driven Contract Management

While AI-driven contract management offers significant advantages, it also presents certain challenges:

Data Privacy and Security: Contracts contain sensitive information, so it's essential to ensure that AI tools adhere to strict data privacy and security standards. Organizations should carefully evaluate vendor policies and take necessary precautions to protect contract data.

Interpreting Complex Legal Language: Despite advances in NLP, some contracts contain nuanced legal language that can be challenging for AI to interpret. In such cases, human oversight remains critical to ensure accurate analysis.

High Initial Investment: Implementing AI-driven contract management tools can involve significant upfront costs, especially for custom solutions. Organizations should evaluate the long-term cost savings and efficiency gains to justify the investment.

Change Management: Transitioning from traditional to AI-driven contract management requires a shift in mindset and processes. Procurement teams need training and support to adapt to new tools and leverage AI's full potential.

7. Real-World Examples of AI-Driven Contract Management in Procurement

Several industries have successfully adopted AI-driven contract management to improve procurement efficiency, compliance, and risk management. Here are a few real-world examples:

Financial Services: Banks and financial institutions use AI to manage contracts with vendors and suppliers, ensuring compliance with regulatory requirements. AI-driven tools help streamline contract reviews, reduce legal risks, and improve response times.

Healthcare: Hospitals and healthcare organizations often deal with complex supplier contracts for medical equipment and pharmaceuticals. AI-powered contract management enables them to track contract terms, ensure compliance, and manage supplier performance effectively.

Retail: Retailers handle numerous supplier contracts for inventory, logistics, and IT services. AI helps them automate contract analysis, identify opportunities for cost savings, and track supplier compliance with delivery schedules.

AI-driven smart contracting is transforming contract management in procurement by automating processes, enhancing accuracy, and enabling proactive risk management. By using AI for contract analysis, risk mitigation, and compliance monitoring, organizations can significantly improve efficiency and reduce risks associated with contract obligations. Smart contracting not only empowers procurement teams to make data-driven decisions but also supports a more agile, strategic approach to managing supplier relationships and compliance requirements. As AI technology continues to advance, smart contracting will play an increasingly vital role in modernizing contract management, ensuring organizations are better equipped to manage complex contracts in today's dynamic business environment.

Part 3: Risk Management and Compliance

Chapter 11: Predictive Risk Analysis in Procurement

Risk management is central to procurement, as organizations must navigate challenges ranging from supplier disruptions and market fluctuations to regulatory compliance. With AI and predictive analytics, procurement teams can proactively identify, assess, and mitigate these risks. Predictive risk analysis leverages historical data, machine learning models, and real-time analytics to forecast potential risks before they impact the supply chain, allowing for informed decision-making and strategic risk mitigation.

In this chapter, we'll explore how predictive risk analysis functions, the applications of AI in risk management, the types of procurement risks that AI can help address, and the benefits of incorporating predictive analytics into procurement.

1. Understanding Predictive Risk Analysis in Procurement

Predictive risk analysis involves using AI and data-driven techniques to predict potential risks and disruptions before they occur. By analyzing historical data, AI can detect patterns and identify signals that indicate possible issues, such as supplier instability, quality concerns, or geopolitical threats. This proactive approach enables procurement teams to make data-backed decisions, plan contingencies, and avoid costly disruptions.

Some essential steps in predictive risk analysis include:

Data Collection and Preprocessing: Gathering relevant data, such as supplier performance, lead times, market trends, and regulatory changes, is critical. This data must be cleaned, categorized, and prepared for analysis.

Identifying Risk Indicators: Predictive models rely on indicators like supplier delivery history, financial stability, compliance records, and external factors such as currency exchange rates or environmental conditions.

Model Development and Training: Machine learning models are developed and trained to recognize patterns associated with specific risks. These models improve over time as they analyze more data, learning to identify subtle indicators of potential issues.

Risk Scoring and Prioritization: Once identified, potential risks are scored based on their severity and likelihood. This allows procurement teams to prioritize high-risk suppliers and take preemptive action where needed.

2. Key Applications of AI in Procurement Risk Management

AI is revolutionizing risk management in procurement by enabling advanced techniques for analyzing and forecasting risks. Here are some ways AI-driven predictive analytics enhances procurement risk management:

Supplier Risk Assessment: AI tools assess supplier performance data, financial stability, and compliance history to predict the likelihood of disruptions. For instance, AI can flag a supplier who consistently fails to meet delivery timelines or has had recent financial setbacks, allowing the procurement team to explore alternative suppliers.

Demand and Supply Chain Disruptions: By analyzing trends in demand, market conditions, and geopolitical factors, AI models can anticipate potential disruptions, such as increased material costs or delays due to political instability. This allows procurement teams to plan inventory levels, negotiate alternative sourcing, or secure strategic partnerships in advance.

Quality Control and Product Risks: Predictive analytics can assess product quality data from past orders to detect patterns that might indicate future quality issues. This is particularly valuable for industries that rely on consistent product standards, such as pharmaceuticals or automotive manufacturing.

Environmental and Regulatory Compliance: AI-driven analytics can monitor regulatory updates and environmental conditions, helping procurement teams comply with evolving standards. For instance, if a supplier operates in an area facing new environmental regulations, predictive analysis can identify the impact on production and help the team plan accordingly.

3. Types of Risks AI Can Address in Procurement

Predictive analytics is highly effective for managing a range of procurement risks, particularly those with quantifiable indicators. The following are common types of procurement risks that AI can help address:

Supplier-Related Risks: Includes risks associated with a supplier's financial health, capacity, and quality. For example, AI can assess whether a supplier's financial history suggests potential bankruptcy or capacity constraints that may cause future delays.

Geopolitical and Market Risks: Risks stemming from political instability, trade policies, or market volatility can be predicted by analyzing data on market trends, currency fluctuations, and import/export policies. AI can provide early warnings for situations that could impact supply chain continuity.

Operational Risks: These risks pertain to disruptions in production, transportation, and delivery. AI can forecast delays by analyzing weather patterns, traffic data, and logistical constraints.

Compliance and Regulatory Risks: With evolving regulations, organizations face the risk of non-compliance. AI helps monitor and predict compliance risks by tracking regulatory changes relevant to suppliers and production regions.

4. Steps to Implement Predictive Risk Analysis in Procurement

Implementing predictive risk analysis in procurement requires a strategic approach that aligns with an organization's goals and resources. The following steps outline the process:

Define Objectives and Scope: Establish clear objectives for predictive risk analysis. Are you focusing on supplier risk, compliance, or overall supply chain resilience? Defining the scope will guide data selection and model development.

Collect and Organize Data: Data is the foundation of predictive risk analysis. Relevant data includes supplier performance history, quality records, delivery times, and external indicators such as political news or weather patterns. Data should be stored and organized for easy access and analysis.

Choose the Right AI and Analytics Tools: Select AI tools that align with your risk analysis goals. Many predictive analytics platforms offer built-in machine learning models, while others may require custom development. Cloud-based solutions can be beneficial for scalability and data security.

Develop and Train Predictive Models: Using historical data, develop machine learning models to identify patterns and predict future risks. Model accuracy improves with data diversity and relevance, so regular updates and training are essential.

Integrate Risk Insights into Procurement Workflows: Ensure that insights generated by predictive models are integrated into procurement workflows. This may involve alerts, dashboards, or risk scoring that allow procurement teams to take timely action.

Monitor and Refine Models: Machine learning models require continuous refinement to remain effective. Regularly evaluate model performance, incorporating feedback from procurement teams and updating data sources as new information becomes available.

5. Benefits of Predictive Risk Analysis in Procurement

Predictive risk analysis provides numerous advantages, allowing procurement teams to proactively manage potential issues and make informed decisions. Key benefits include:

Proactive Risk Mitigation: By identifying risks in advance, procurement teams can take preventative actions, such as seeking alternative suppliers or adjusting inventory levels, to minimize disruption.

Enhanced Supplier Relationships: Identifying potential issues early enables procurement teams to collaborate with suppliers on corrective actions, strengthening relationships and fostering a culture of transparency and accountability.

Cost Savings: Proactive risk management reduces costs associated with supply chain disruptions, such as emergency sourcing, production delays, or compliance penalties.

Informed Decision-Making: Predictive risk analysis provides data-backed insights that empower procurement professionals to make informed decisions, reducing reliance on reactive strategies and guesswork.

Improved Supply Chain Resilience: By anticipating and mitigating risks, organizations can build a more resilient supply chain capable of adapting to dynamic conditions, such as changing market demands or regulatory environments.

6. Challenges and Considerations in Implementing Predictive Risk Analysis

While predictive risk analysis offers transformative potential, there are several challenges and considerations to keep in mind:

Data Quality and Availability: Predictive models rely on accurate, relevant data, which can be difficult to obtain. Organizations must prioritize data quality and establish reliable data sources for effective risk analysis.

Model Interpretability: Some machine learning models, especially complex algorithms, can be challenging to interpret. Procurement teams must understand how predictions are generated to trust the insights and make effective decisions.

Initial Investment and Resources: Implementing predictive risk analysis requires investment in technology, data infrastructure, and training. Organizations should assess the potential ROI to justify these costs.

Privacy and Security Concerns: Data privacy is paramount, especially when handling sensitive supplier or market data. Organizations should ensure compliance with data protection regulations and implement robust security measures.

Change Management: Transitioning to AI-driven risk analysis requires buy-in from procurement teams and stakeholders. Proper training and communication are essential to foster adoption and ensure smooth integration into existing workflows.

7. Real-World Applications of Predictive Risk Analysis in Procurement

Several industries have adopted predictive risk analysis to mitigate procurement risks effectively. Here are a few real-world examples:

Automotive: Automakers rely on a vast network of suppliers for parts and materials. AI-driven risk analysis helps them monitor supplier stability and manage risks associated with critical parts, ensuring uninterrupted production.

Retail: Retailers use predictive analytics to forecast demand changes, manage supplier risks, and address potential disruptions in logistics. This has helped major retailers avoid stockouts during peak seasons and optimize inventory levels.

Healthcare: In the healthcare industry, supply chain continuity is vital for patient care. Hospitals and medical facilities use predictive risk analysis to identify potential supply shortages and ensure timely delivery of critical medical supplies.

Predictive risk analysis is reshaping procurement risk management by empowering organizations to anticipate and address risks before they escalate. By leveraging AI to assess supplier stability, demand fluctuations, regulatory shifts, and other risk factors, procurement teams can make proactive, data-driven decisions that safeguard the supply chain.

The integration of predictive analytics enables procurement professionals to move beyond traditional, reactive approaches and toward a more strategic, resilient procurement process. While there are challenges to consider, the benefits of predictive risk analysis—including cost savings, improved supplier relationships, and enhanced resilience—make it a valuable asset in today's dynamic procurement landscape. As AI continues to advance, predictive risk analysis will become an indispensable tool for building a secure, adaptable, and efficient procurement function.

Chapter 12: Ensuring Compliance through AI and ML

Compliance is a crucial aspect of procurement, encompassing adherence to legal, regulatory, and internal standards to protect an organization's reputation, ensure legal safety, and promote ethical business practices. The complexity and volume of regulations in procurement—ranging from environmental laws and labor practices to financial and trade compliance—can make compliance management time-consuming and prone to errors if handled manually. This is where AI and Machine Learning (ML) bring transformational potential, automating compliance checks and monitoring regulatory adherence with unprecedented accuracy and efficiency.

In this chapter, we will delve into the role of AI and ML in compliance within procurement, key applications of AI-driven compliance automation, benefits of using AI for compliance, and challenges in implementation.

1. The Role of AI and ML in Procurement Compliance

AI and ML technologies offer new avenues for streamlining compliance in procurement. By automating data analysis, compliance checks, and regulatory monitoring, AI enables procurement teams to ensure ongoing adherence to complex standards while minimizing human error. ML models can be trained to detect anomalies, flag potential compliance violations, and even predict areas where future compliance risks may arise.

Key compliance areas where AI and ML can be highly effective include:

Supplier Compliance: Monitoring supplier adherence to standards, such as ethical labor practices, environmental regulations, and financial integrity.

Contract Compliance: Ensuring that contract terms are adhered to throughout the procurement lifecycle.

Data Privacy Compliance: Ensuring that procurement data, including supplier information, is managed and stored in line with data protection laws.

Trade and Financial Compliance: Adhering to trade regulations, tax requirements, and anti-corruption laws.

2. Applications of AI-Driven Compliance in Procurement

AI and ML provide powerful tools for various applications in procurement compliance, automating everything from supplier evaluation to monitoring regulatory changes. Here are some of the primary applications:

Automated Supplier Compliance Verification: AI-driven solutions can analyze supplier data and verify compliance with standards like certifications, environmental policies, and labor practices. With ML, these systems learn from past compliance data, improving their ability to flag non-compliant suppliers over time. For instance, a procurement team might use AI to automatically scan suppliers' environmental impact reports, flagging those that don't meet specific benchmarks.

Contract Analysis and Monitoring: Natural language processing (NLP) algorithms allow AI to review contracts for terms and conditions that might pose compliance risks. ML can monitor ongoing contract performance, alerting teams if terms aren't being met or if there's a deviation from agreed compliance standards. This is particularly valuable for long-term contracts with intricate terms that are hard to monitor manually.

Regulatory Change Tracking: Regulatory landscapes are always shifting, with new laws or amendments often impacting procurement practices. AI can monitor legal databases, government publications, and industry news sources to detect regulatory changes relevant to procurement and send alerts to the procurement team. This ensures that organizations remain up-to-date and compliant without needing to rely solely on manual updates.

Real-Time Transaction Monitoring: AI can monitor procurement transactions in real time, analyzing patterns for potential fraud, errors, or regulatory violations. Machine learning models, especially those trained on historical data, can detect anomalies—such as unusually high spending on specific items or uncharacteristic purchase volumes—that may indicate non-compliance or fraud.

Automated Compliance Audits: Routine audits are essential for demonstrating compliance, but they are often resource-intensive. AI can automate portions of the auditing process, analyzing procurement records, supplier contracts, and transactions for compliance adherence. This automation reduces the time required for audits and enhances audit accuracy.

3. Benefits of AI in Compliance Automation

Using AI to ensure compliance in procurement delivers numerous advantages:

Enhanced Accuracy: AI algorithms can process vast amounts of data with precision, reducing the likelihood of human error in compliance checks. For example, AI-driven contract analysis can spot subtle discrepancies that might be overlooked manually.

Increased Efficiency: AI automates repetitive compliance tasks, allowing procurement teams to focus on strategic initiatives. By reducing manual reviews and checks, AI cuts down the time needed for compliance tasks, leading to faster procurement cycles and better resource allocation.

Proactive Compliance Management: AI enables organizations to proactively manage compliance by detecting potential risks early. For instance, by identifying trends in regulatory changes or by monitoring shifts in supplier performance, AI allows procurement teams to address compliance issues before they become costly problems.

Reduced Compliance Costs: Automating compliance activities can lead to significant cost savings by decreasing the need for extensive human oversight and reducing the potential for fines or legal fees due to non-compliance. AI-powered compliance tools are scalable, offering greater coverage at lower costs.

Scalability: As an organization grows, managing compliance becomes increasingly challenging. AI can easily scale with the organization, handling larger volumes of data and more suppliers without requiring additional resources.

4. Implementing AI and ML for Compliance in Procurement

Implementing AI-driven compliance solutions requires careful planning, as well as collaboration with legal, IT, and procurement teams. Here are essential steps for integrating AI into compliance processes:

Define Compliance Goals and Requirements: Establish specific goals for AI in compliance, such as tracking supplier ethics, adhering to environmental standards, or ensuring trade compliance. Clear objectives guide the selection of AI tools and models.

Select Appropriate AI Tools and Solutions: Numerous AI solutions focus on compliance in procurement, including contract management software, real-time monitoring tools, and regulatory alert systems. Choose tools that align with your compliance goals and budget.

Ensure Data Availability and Quality: AI-driven compliance is heavily dependent on data quality. Ensure that procurement records, supplier data, and transaction histories are accurately recorded and structured. Using clean, comprehensive data will improve model accuracy and ensure meaningful compliance checks.

Train and Monitor ML Models: Training machine learning models requires historical data on compliance performance, both for compliant and non-compliant cases. It's also crucial to continually update and retrain models to incorporate the latest regulatory information and evolving procurement practices.

Integrate AI Insights into Procurement Workflows: To be effective, AI-driven compliance insights should be embedded in procurement processes. For example, alerts about non-compliance should be integrated into procurement systems so that users can see and act on them in real time.

Regularly Audit AI Systems for Accuracy and Fairness: Over time, it's essential to audit AI compliance systems to ensure they're accurate and unbiased. Regular audits will maintain model integrity and identify areas for improvement.

5. Challenges and Considerations in AI-Driven Compliance

While AI-driven compliance provides numerous benefits, there are some challenges and considerations to keep in mind:

Data Privacy and Security: Compliance data often includes sensitive information, such as supplier financials and contract terms. Ensuring data privacy and security is essential to prevent breaches and maintain regulatory compliance, especially with laws like GDPR.

Model Interpretability: Some AI models, particularly complex ML algorithms, may produce results that are challenging to interpret. Ensuring that procurement teams understand the rationale behind AI-generated compliance alerts is critical for gaining trust in AI recommendations.

Integration with Legacy Systems: Many procurement teams work with legacy systems that may not seamlessly integrate with modern AI tools. Proper planning and possible system upgrades may be necessary for effective implementation.

Maintaining Up-to-Date Regulatory Information: Regulatory changes are constant, and AI models need up-to-date information to stay effective. Organizations must establish a reliable way of feeding new regulatory information into AI models, whether through data subscriptions or partnerships with legal experts.

Managing False Positives: AI-driven compliance systems can sometimes generate false positives, which can overwhelm procurement teams with alerts. Training models to distinguish genuine compliance risks from harmless anomalies requires careful model refinement.

6. Real-World Applications of AI in Compliance Automation

Numerous companies are already leveraging AI to streamline compliance in procurement. Here are a few examples:

Retail Industry: Retailers face strict product and supplier compliance standards, especially in areas like safety and labor practices. AI tools in retail procurement scan supplier records and monitor social media for any potential violations, helping retailers manage compliance with minimal manual intervention.

Pharmaceuticals: Pharmaceutical companies use AI-driven compliance tools to adhere to stringent regulatory standards for supplier quality and product safety. By automating contract checks and monitoring regulatory updates, these companies ensure compliance while reducing operational overhead.

Financial Services: Financial institutions leverage AI to comply with complex procurement regulations, particularly in supplier relationships and transaction monitoring. AI tools flag unusual procurement patterns that could indicate non-compliance, improving regulatory adherence in this highly regulated industry.

7. The Future of AI-Driven Compliance in Procurement

As AI technology advances, its role in compliance will continue to expand, with emerging capabilities likely to include:

Predictive Compliance: Future AI systems will not only detect compliance issues but also predict potential risks based on historical data and emerging patterns. For example, an AI system might warn procurement teams about potential compliance issues with new suppliers even before contracts are signed.

Increased Use of Blockchain for Compliance Verification: The combination of AI and blockchain technology can enhance compliance by offering transparent, tamper-proof records of procurement transactions. Blockchain could store supplier certifications and contract terms in a secure, accessible format that AI models can easily analyze for compliance.

Improved Ethical Compliance Monitoring: As consumers and stakeholders increasingly demand ethical sourcing, AI models will incorporate metrics that monitor not only regulatory compliance but also adherence to ethical standards in labor, environmental impact, and corporate social responsibility.

AI and ML are transforming compliance in procurement, offering powerful tools to automate and enhance regulatory adherence. From monitoring supplier compliance to ensuring that contracts are executed within legal parameters, AI simplifies the compliance process and mitigates the risk of non-compliance. While implementation requires investment in data management, system integration, and model training, the benefits—greater accuracy, efficiency, and scalability—make AI a valuable asset for any procurement team aiming to navigate today's complex compliance landscape.

Chapter 13: AI-Enhanced Fraud Detection and Prevention

Procurement fraud is a significant challenge for organizations, impacting finances, reputation, and operational efficiency. Fraud in procurement can occur at various stages, including supplier selection, contract negotiation, invoicing, and payment processing. Traditional fraud detection methods often rely on manual audits, which can be time-consuming, prone to human error, and limited in their capacity to detect sophisticated fraud patterns. Artificial Intelligence (AI) and Machine Learning (ML) bring a revolutionary approach to fraud detection and prevention, allowing organizations to analyze vast amounts of data and detect anomalies in real time.

In this chapter, we will explore how AI can be used to detect and prevent fraud in procurement, including its applications, benefits, key strategies for implementation, and challenges.

1. Understanding Procurement Fraud and Its Implications

Procurement fraud encompasses a wide range of activities that result in financial losses and operational inefficiencies. Key types of procurement fraud include:

Bid Rigging: When suppliers collude to inflate bids or create a false appearance of competition, often leading to inflated prices and losses for the purchasing organization.

Invoice Fraud: Involves submitting duplicate, inflated, or fake invoices for payment, often through misrepresentation or false billing.

Supplier Kickbacks: Occurs when procurement personnel receive kickbacks or bribes in exchange for awarding contracts to specific suppliers.

Collusion and Conflicts of Interest: When procurement staff have undisclosed relationships with suppliers, leading to biased selection and potential overpricing.

Phantom Suppliers: Involves creating fake suppliers or vendors to divert funds through fictitious invoices and payments.

These types of fraud not only harm the financial health of organizations but also damage relationships with stakeholders, impede competitive procurement practices, and jeopardize legal compliance.

2. Role of AI in Fraud Detection and Prevention

AI enhances fraud detection by automating the analysis of procurement transactions, identifying patterns that may indicate fraudulent activity, and providing real-time alerts to procurement teams. Machine learning models can be trained to recognize suspicious behavior, allowing organizations to detect and prevent fraud with greater accuracy and efficiency than manual methods.

AI's key roles in fraud detection and prevention include:

Pattern Recognition: AI algorithms can analyze historical transaction data to identify normal patterns and detect deviations that might signal fraud. For example, if an employee consistently selects the same supplier regardless of price or quality, this could indicate a conflict of interest.

Anomaly Detection: By setting a baseline for typical procurement behavior, AI can detect anomalies, such as unusually high expenses or payments to unapproved vendors, which may indicate fraudulent activity.

Predictive Analysis: Using machine learning, AI systems can predict potential fraud based on past data, helping organizations take preventive actions before fraud occurs.

Behavioral Analysis: AI can analyze user behavior, such as changes in procurement patterns, to identify activities that deviate from expected behavior. For example, if a procurement employee's actions suddenly differ from established norms, AI can flag this change for review.

3. Applications of AI in Procurement Fraud Detection

AI can be applied in various ways to enhance fraud detection and prevention in procurement:

Real-Time Transaction Monitoring: AI enables real-time monitoring of procurement transactions, identifying suspicious transactions instantly. Machine learning models are trained to detect fraud indicators, such as unusually high invoice amounts or sudden increases in the frequency of purchases from specific suppliers. Real-time alerts allow procurement teams to take immediate action, reducing potential losses.

Supplier Verification and Vetting: AI can streamline the vetting process by verifying supplier information, checking for discrepancies in supplier data, and analyzing financial health indicators to assess potential fraud risks. By automating this process, AI reduces the likelihood of onboarding phantom suppliers or unqualified vendors.

Duplicate Invoice Detection: Machine learning algorithms can identify duplicate invoices submitted for payment, one of the most common types of procurement fraud. By comparing invoice details, such as supplier names, amounts, and dates, AI can detect duplicates even when minor modifications are made to avoid detection.

Conflict of Interest Detection: AI can analyze relationships between procurement personnel and suppliers to detect potential conflicts of interest. By examining procurement records, email communications, and supplier databases, AI can identify patterns that might suggest collusion or favoritism.

Expense and Budget Monitoring: AI can help procurement teams manage expenses by tracking budget allocations and flagging spending that exceeds thresholds or deviates from expected norms. This type of oversight can help detect fraudulent spending and prevent unauthorized purchases.

Advanced Contract Analysis: Using Natural Language Processing (NLP), AI can analyze contract language to identify clauses or terms that deviate from standard practices, which may indicate fraudulent intent. AI can also review contract amendments for unusual changes that could benefit specific parties inappropriately.

4. Benefits of AI-Driven Fraud Detection in Procurement

Implementing AI for fraud detection provides numerous benefits for organizations:

Increased Accuracy and Speed: AI's ability to process large volumes of data quickly and accurately enables it to detect fraud with far greater speed than traditional manual methods. For instance, AI can analyze millions of invoices in seconds, flagging fraudulent ones instantly.

Reduction in Financial Losses: By detecting fraud in its early stages, AI minimizes the financial impact on the organization. Real-time alerts and rapid fraud detection reduce the duration of fraud, leading to less monetary loss and quicker resolutions.

Enhanced Audit Capabilities: AI-powered fraud detection improves audit processes by automating the review of procurement records, transactions, and supplier relationships. This reduces the burden on audit teams and enhances the thoroughness and accuracy of audits.

Prevention of Reputational Damage: Detecting and preventing fraud protects an organization's reputation by ensuring ethical practices and accountability in procurement. A reputation for stringent fraud prevention attracts more reputable suppliers and builds trust with stakeholders.

Increased Compliance: AI supports regulatory compliance by detecting activities that violate procurement policies and regulatory requirements, reducing the risk of fines or legal action.

5. Implementing AI for Fraud Detection in Procurement

Successfully implementing AI for fraud detection requires a structured approach:

Define Fraud Detection Goals: Identify the primary types of procurement fraud your organization wants to detect and outline the specific fraud detection capabilities needed, such as real-time monitoring or anomaly detection.

Choose the Right AI Tools and Vendors: Select AI tools designed for fraud detection, with features like anomaly detection, supplier verification, and transaction monitoring. Evaluate vendors based on their ability to integrate with existing procurement systems and provide customizable fraud detection algorithms.

Ensure Data Quality and Integration: Quality data is essential for accurate fraud detection. Clean, complete, and accessible data from procurement records, supplier databases, and transaction histories should be available for AI algorithms to analyze effectively.

Train and Test Machine Learning Models: Use historical fraud data to train ML models, allowing them to learn from past fraud cases. Testing the models in a controlled environment helps ensure they are effective in detecting fraud patterns before deployment.

Develop a Response Protocol for Alerts: Establish a clear protocol for responding to fraud alerts generated by AI, including investigation steps, corrective actions, and escalation procedures. This ensures that procurement teams are prepared to handle alerts efficiently.

Monitor and Update Models Regularly: As fraud patterns evolve, it's essential to retrain and update ML models to reflect new fraud techniques and trends. Regular updates ensure that fraud detection capabilities remain accurate and relevant.

6. Challenges in AI-Driven Fraud Detection

While AI brings numerous advantages to fraud detection, there are also challenges to consider:

False Positives: AI-driven fraud detection systems can generate false positives, alerting on transactions that are not fraudulent. This can create additional work for procurement teams. Continuous refinement and model training are necessary to reduce false positives.

Complexity of Model Interpretability: Some AI models, particularly deep learning algorithms, may act as "black boxes," providing fraud alerts without clear explanations. Ensuring transparency and interpretability in model output is important for gaining trust and enabling effective responses to fraud alerts.

Data Privacy and Security: Fraud detection systems rely on access to sensitive procurement data, including transactions and supplier details. Organizations must ensure that data privacy and security measures are in place to prevent unauthorized access.

Integration with Legacy Systems: Many organizations still use legacy procurement systems that may be difficult to integrate with AI tools. Ensuring compatibility or upgrading systems may be necessary for effective AI deployment.

Skilled Personnel Requirements: Implementing AI-driven fraud detection may require staff with technical expertise in data science and AI. Training procurement teams to understand and manage AI systems is essential for successful implementation.

7. Case Examples of AI in Procurement Fraud Detection

Several organizations have successfully implemented AI-driven fraud detection systems to secure their procurement processes:

Government Agencies: Government procurement departments use AI to monitor large-scale contracts and detect bid rigging, reducing costs and improving transparency. By analyzing bidding patterns, AI can detect potential collusion among suppliers and alert teams for further investigation.

Manufacturing Industry: Manufacturers leverage AI to monitor supply chain expenses and flag unusual spending patterns, preventing duplicate billing and identifying phantom suppliers. This has led to significant cost savings and enhanced compliance with internal procurement policies.

Retail Sector: Retail companies use AI to detect fraud in purchase orders and invoices, helping to minimize losses from invoice fraud and unauthorized purchases. By implementing AI-driven real-time monitoring, these organizations have reduced financial losses and improved procurement accuracy.

8. The Future of AI-Enhanced Fraud Detection in Procurement

The future of AI-driven fraud detection will likely include several advancements:

Predictive Fraud Detection: Future AI models will not only detect fraud but also predict potential fraud risks based on patterns and trends. For example, AI could identify suppliers with a high likelihood of engaging in fraud based on historical behavior and industry insights.

Blockchain Integration: Integrating blockchain with AI could enhance fraud detection by creating transparent and immutable procurement records. Blockchain can help verify supplier identities and create secure, tamper-resistant records of transactions.

Increased Use of NLP for Behavioral Insights: Natural Language Processing (NLP) advancements will improve AI's ability to analyze unstructured data, such as emails and social media, to detect potential conflicts of interest or unethical behavior among suppliers and procurement teams.

In conclusion, AI-driven fraud detection provides procurement teams with a powerful tool to detect and prevent fraudulent activity, enhancing financial security, operational efficiency, and compliance. As AI technology continues to advance, organizations will benefit from increasingly sophisticated fraud detection capabilities, allowing them to protect their resources and uphold ethical procurement practices.

Part 4: Automation and Process Optimization

Chapter 14: Automating Routine Procurement Tasks

Procurement processes are complex, requiring considerable time and resources to manage activities like purchase orders, invoicing, and vendor communications. Routine tasks, while necessary, can be time-consuming and prone to human error. Automation through Artificial Intelligence (AI) and advanced digital tools is revolutionizing how procurement teams manage these activities, streamlining workflows, and allowing professionals to focus on higher-value strategic initiatives.

This chapter explores how automation improves procurement efficiency, reduces costs, minimizes errors, and enables a more agile and responsive procurement function.

1. Overview of Routine Tasks in Procurement

Routine tasks in procurement are repetitive activities that ensure the continuous flow of goods and services necessary for daily operations. Key examples of routine tasks include:

Purchase Order (PO) Creation: Generating POs for goods and services to document and authorize orders.

Invoice Processing: Managing invoices received from suppliers, matching them to purchase orders, and ensuring accuracy for payments.

Supplier Onboarding: Collecting and verifying supplier details, contracts, and compliance documentation.

Order Tracking and Follow-ups: Monitoring the status of orders and following up with suppliers to ensure timely delivery.

Document Management: Handling large volumes of paperwork, such as contracts, invoices, and shipping documents, essential for record-keeping and compliance.

These tasks, though critical, often consume a significant portion of procurement teams' time, leading to inefficiencies, delays, and reduced productivity. Automation addresses these challenges by taking over repetitive tasks and allowing procurement professionals to focus on higher-level responsibilities.

2. Benefits of Automating Routine Procurement Tasks

Automating routine procurement tasks yields a wide range of benefits, from time savings to enhanced compliance. Here are some key advantages of automating these tasks:

Time and Cost Savings: Automation reduces the time required to complete repetitive tasks, like generating POs and processing invoices. For example, automated invoice processing eliminates the need for manual data entry, reducing labor costs and accelerating payment cycles.

Minimized Errors: Human errors, such as data entry mistakes or incorrect pricing, can lead to costly rework and supplier disputes. Automation minimizes these errors by ensuring consistent data entry and validation, improving overall accuracy.

Improved Compliance and Documentation: Automated systems provide audit trails, automatically recording every transaction, which enhances compliance with regulations and internal policies. Automated document management also ensures that records are accurate, accessible, and well-organized.

Enhanced Supplier Relationships: By reducing the time needed to process orders and invoices, automation enables faster and more reliable interactions with suppliers. This helps improve supplier relationships, as suppliers experience fewer delays and more transparent communications.

Increased Productivity: With routine tasks handled by automation, procurement teams can dedicate more time to strategic tasks, such as supplier negotiations, spend analysis, and risk management, leading to improved decision-making.

Scalability: Automation allows procurement functions to scale up their operations without requiring additional personnel. For example, as a company grows and procurement demands increase, automated processes can handle higher volumes with minimal adjustments.

3. Automation Tools for Routine Procurement Tasks

Several automation tools and technologies are available to streamline procurement tasks. The most commonly used tools include:

Robotic Process Automation (RPA): RPA uses software "robots" to automate repetitive tasks by mimicking human actions. RPA can be used to copy data from emails, extract information from invoices, and enter data into procurement systems, reducing manual effort significantly.

Intelligent Document Processing (IDP): IDP combines AI with Optical Character Recognition (OCR) to read and process documents like invoices and POs. This technology extracts data from structured and unstructured documents, allowing seamless integration with procurement systems.

Automated Purchase Order Systems: PO automation tools create and approve purchase orders based on pre-defined rules and thresholds. These systems automatically generate POs when stock levels reach a certain point or when a purchase request is approved.

Automated Invoice Processing Software: Automated invoice processing tools match invoices with purchase orders and receipts to validate payments, enabling faster and more accurate processing. For example, software can flag discrepancies in amounts or duplicate invoices for review.

Supplier Portals: Supplier portals allow suppliers to upload their documents, submit invoices, and track order status. This reduces the time procurement teams spend managing supplier communications, as suppliers can independently access relevant information.

Workflow Automation Tools: Workflow automation platforms, such as ERP systems with procurement modules, streamline approval workflows, ensuring that tasks like PO approvals or budget verifications are routed to the right person automatically.

4. Applications of Automation in Routine Procurement Tasks

Automation can be applied to a wide range of procurement tasks, transforming how procurement teams operate. Here's a closer look at specific tasks that benefit from automation:

Purchase Order (PO) Automation: Automated systems can generate POs based on triggers such as stock levels, budget availability, or previous order history. When a PO is generated, it is automatically routed for approval, reducing time spent on manual PO creation. Once approved, the PO is sent to the supplier automatically, speeding up the ordering process.

Invoice Automation: Invoices from suppliers can be automatically processed using OCR and machine learning to capture essential data. Automated systems match invoices to POs and receipts, identifying any discrepancies and flagging them for review. This eliminates the need for manual data entry and accelerates payment cycles.

Supplier Onboarding Automation: Supplier onboarding can be a time-intensive process involving data collection, verification, and documentation. Automated onboarding platforms streamline these tasks by allowing suppliers to upload their own documents, which are then verified using AI algorithms. Automated compliance checks also ensure suppliers meet regulatory requirements.

Order Tracking and Management: Automation tools can track order status in real time, sending updates and alerts to procurement teams and suppliers as the order progresses. If a delay or issue occurs, automated alerts prompt procurement professionals to take corrective actions, ensuring timely delivery.

Contract Management: Automation streamlines contract creation, approval, and renewal. Smart contracts, for instance, can be programmed with terms that trigger payments or renewals automatically when certain conditions are met. Automated contract management reduces administrative burdens and helps avoid missed renewals.

Budget and Spend Management: Automated tools track budgets and alert procurement teams when spending approaches predefined limits. This allows organizations to stay within budget and make real-time adjustments based on spending trends.

5. Case Studies in Procurement Task Automation

Many organizations have successfully adopted automation to optimize procurement processes. Here are a few examples:

117

Retail Company - Invoice Automation: A large retailer implemented automated invoice processing to reduce manual data entry and errors. With AI-powered invoice processing, the retailer achieved a 40% reduction in invoice processing time and a 25% reduction in payment errors.

Manufacturing Firm - Purchase Order Automation: A manufacturing firm automated its PO creation process, which significantly reduced the time required to generate and approve POs. By setting automated reorder points, the company prevented stockouts, improved supplier relationships, and saved over 200 hours of manual work annually.

Healthcare Provider - Supplier Onboarding: A healthcare provider streamlined its supplier onboarding process by using automation to verify supplier credentials, licenses, and compliance documentation. This improved supplier vetting efficiency by 60% and reduced the risk of non-compliant suppliers entering the network.

6. Steps to Implement Automation in Routine Procurement Tasks

Implementing automation in procurement requires careful planning and a structured approach to ensure effectiveness and minimize disruptions:

Assess Automation Needs: Identify the specific tasks that could benefit the most from automation. This might include high-volume tasks like invoice processing, order tracking, or supplier onboarding.

Define Goals and Objectives: Set clear objectives, such as reducing processing times, minimizing errors, or enhancing supplier communication. These goals will guide the selection of automation tools and success metrics.

Select Automation Tools: Choose the right automation tools based on the tasks identified, budget, and compatibility with existing procurement systems. Consider tools with robust integration capabilities and user-friendly interfaces.

Integrate with Existing Systems: Ensure that the chosen automation tools integrate seamlessly with existing procurement, ERP, or accounting systems to facilitate smooth data flow.

Train Procurement Teams: Training is essential to ensure that teams understand how to use the new systems effectively. Training should cover not only technical skills but also how to manage and interpret automated alerts.

Monitor and Optimize: Once automation is in place, continuously monitor its performance to identify any bottlenecks or issues. Regular updates and optimizations can help keep automation aligned with procurement goals.

7. Challenges of Automating Procurement Tasks

While automation brings many benefits, it also presents challenges that organizations must address for successful implementation:

Initial Costs and Resource Allocation: Implementing automation can require a significant upfront investment, particularly for advanced AI and RPA systems. Organizations should be prepared to allocate resources for initial setup and ongoing maintenance.

Data Privacy and Security: Automated systems process sensitive procurement data, which may include supplier information and financial records. Ensuring robust data security and privacy measures is essential to protect against data breaches.

Resistance to Change: Procurement teams may be hesitant to adopt new systems, especially if they are accustomed to manual processes. Organizations should manage change by communicating the benefits of automation and providing training to ease the transition.

Dependence on Data Quality: Automation relies on accurate, high-quality data to function effectively. Poor data quality can lead to errors, inefficiencies, and ineffective automation outcomes.

8. Future of Procurement Task Automation

The future of procurement automation will likely involve further advancements in AI, such as machine learning for predictive analytics and natural language processing (NLP) for improved document processing and communication. Additionally, as technologies like blockchain become more integrated into procurement, automation could be extended to cover even more complex tasks, such as smart contract execution and decentralized supplier verification.

Automation of routine procurement tasks offers immense potential to enhance efficiency, accuracy, and cost-effectiveness. By automating activities like PO creation, invoice processing, and supplier onboarding, organizations can reduce operational burdens and focus on strategic initiatives that drive long-term value. With careful planning, the right tools, and ongoing optimization, procurement teams can leverage automation to become more agile, resilient, and prepared for the future of procurement.

Chapter 15: AI-Driven Workflow and Process Efficiency

Modern procurement functions are under pressure to manage an increasing number of tasks with higher levels of accuracy and speed. As procurement teams strive to deliver goods and services promptly while minimizing costs, optimizing workflows becomes essential. Traditional process improvements may only address part of the problem, which is where Artificial Intelligence (AI) steps in to fundamentally reshape how procurement workflows operate. AI-driven workflow optimization helps organizations streamline processes, increase accuracy, and accelerate task completion, contributing directly to more strategic and effective procurement management.

This chapter delves into how AI-driven workflow optimization improves procurement processes, enhances productivity, and fosters a more agile and responsive procurement environment.

1. Understanding AI-Driven Workflow Optimization in Procurement

AI-driven workflow optimization involves using AI tools to analyze, manage, and improve workflows in procurement. Traditional workflow management relies on manually defined rules and sequential task assignments, but AI allows workflows to adapt dynamically based on real-time data, predictive analytics, and automation capabilities. This shift empowers procurement teams to manage complex tasks more efficiently, as AI can rapidly detect inefficiencies, predict bottlenecks, and suggest or initiate improvements.

Some key AI-driven optimization techniques include:

Process Automation: AI automates repetitive tasks, such as purchase order generation or invoice matching, freeing up procurement staff for more strategic work.

Predictive Analytics: AI uses data to predict potential issues, such as supplier delays or stock shortages, allowing teams to act proactively.

Smart Task Allocation: AI-driven systems can assign tasks to team members based on current workloads, expertise, and task priority, optimizing team performance.

Real-Time Monitoring: AI tracks ongoing workflows, identifying and correcting inefficiencies in real time.

2. Benefits of AI-Driven Workflow Optimization in Procurement

Optimizing workflows through AI brings several substantial benefits to procurement operations:

Enhanced Speed and Efficiency: AI can dramatically reduce processing times for routine tasks, such as approvals and document handling. With

AI, what might take hours or days in traditional workflows can be completed within minutes.

Increased Accuracy and Consistency: AI helps standardize workflows, reducing the likelihood of errors, especially in tasks like data entry or compliance checks. By automating checks and validations, AI enhances consistency across procurement tasks.

Improved Decision-Making: By analyzing historical data and predicting trends, AI provides valuable insights that help procurement teams make faster and more informed decisions. For example, AI can recommend optimal reorder points based on demand patterns and lead times.

Scalability: AI-driven workflows can scale to accommodate increasing volumes without significant changes to existing systems. As organizations grow, AI ensures procurement functions can handle more transactions and suppliers without compromising efficiency.

Real-Time Performance Monitoring: AI provides real-time insights into workflow performance, helping procurement leaders to address issues proactively and make adjustments that enhance team productivity.

3. Key Areas of Workflow Optimization in Procurement

There are several procurement functions where AI-driven workflow optimization can have the most significant impact. These include:

Purchase Order Processing: Traditionally, creating and approving purchase orders (POs) involves multiple steps and manual verification. AI optimizes this workflow by automating PO generation, approval routing, and validation. By analyzing historical PO data, AI can also suggest optimal order quantities and timing.

Supplier Onboarding and Management: Supplier onboarding typically requires verification of documentation, regulatory compliance, and contractual terms. AI expedites onboarding by automatically validating supplier data, cross-referencing with regulatory databases, and setting up continuous monitoring for compliance. For supplier management, AI-driven tools streamline communication, track performance, and automate risk assessments.

Invoice Matching and Processing: AI improves invoice processing by automating data extraction, matching invoices to purchase orders, and flagging discrepancies for review. This approach reduces manual invoice handling time, decreases the risk of payment delays, and enhances overall accuracy.

Approval Workflows: Many procurement tasks require approvals from multiple stakeholders. AI-driven workflows streamline this process by automatically routing approvals based on predefined criteria, reminding approvers of pending tasks, and escalating overdue approvals to maintain operational efficiency.

Contract Management: AI can manage the entire contract lifecycle, from drafting and reviewing to monitoring compliance and renewal. AI-driven contract management tools analyze contract terms, suggest revisions, and alert procurement teams to upcoming renewal dates, reducing administrative burdens and enhancing compliance.

4. Tools and Technologies for AI-Driven Workflow Optimization

Several AI tools and technologies support workflow optimization in procurement, offering various levels of customization, automation, and analytical capabilities:

Robotic Process Automation (RPA): RPA automates routine tasks, such as data entry, order processing, and invoice matching, by mimicking human actions. Although not AI in itself, RPA integrates with AI tools to provide even greater efficiency by handling repetitive processes automatically.

Machine Learning Algorithms: Machine learning algorithms analyze historical procurement data to predict outcomes and suggest improvements. For instance, predictive models can determine optimal order timing based on historical supplier performance and demand trends.

Natural Language Processing (NLP): NLP enables AI systems to process and interpret textual data, such as emails, contracts, and supplier communications. This helps procurement teams automate responses to inquiries, flag contract risks, and even assess sentiment in supplier feedback.

Process Mining Tools: Process mining tools analyze event logs to identify inefficiencies, deviations, and bottlenecks in workflows. By mapping out actual workflows, these tools provide valuable insights into areas where AI-driven optimization can improve speed and accuracy.

AI-Powered Procurement Platforms: Many modern procurement platforms come equipped with AI capabilities, such as smart approvals, automated document handling, and predictive analytics, that are specifically designed to optimize procurement workflows.

5. AI in Action: Practical Examples of Workflow Optimization

AI-driven workflow optimization can bring tangible improvements to procurement. Here are a few real-world examples demonstrating how AI enhances workflow efficiency:

Automated Approval Processes at a Global Manufacturing Firm: A global manufacturing company used AI-driven approval workflows to reduce delays in PO approvals. The system automatically routed approvals based on order value and urgency, and sent reminders for pending tasks. The result was a 35% reduction in approval cycle times, enabling the firm to complete orders faster and strengthen supplier relationships.

Predictive Inventory Management for a Retail Chain: A retail chain implemented AI-driven predictive analytics to optimize reorder timing and prevent stockouts. By analyzing historical sales data and supplier lead times, the AI system recommended order quantities and schedules that minimized stockouts by 20% and reduced inventory holding costs by 15%.

Streamlined Invoice Processing in a Healthcare Provider: A healthcare provider automated its invoice matching process, significantly reducing the time required to validate and approve invoices. Using OCR and AI algorithms, the system extracted data from invoices and matched it to purchase orders with over 95% accuracy, allowing the provider to process 40% more invoices without adding staff.

6. Implementing AI-Driven Workflow Optimization in Procurement

Implementing AI-driven workflow optimization requires careful planning to ensure the technology is well-suited to the organization's needs and integrated smoothly with existing processes. Here are the key steps for a successful implementation:

Identify Key Areas for Automation: Begin by mapping current procurement workflows to identify repetitive and time-intensive tasks that would benefit most from AI-driven optimization.

Set Objectives and KPIs: Define what the organization aims to achieve through workflow optimization, such as reduced processing times, improved accuracy, or increased productivity. Set measurable KPIs to track progress.

Select Appropriate AI Tools: Choose AI tools that align with your organization's workflow needs. Evaluate options based on ease of integration, customization, and user-friendliness, and ensure compatibility with current procurement and ERP systems.

Ensure Data Quality: AI relies on accurate data to deliver effective results. Ensure that data sources, such as supplier information and transaction records, are clean, standardized, and regularly updated.

Train Procurement Teams: Comprehensive training ensures that team members understand how to use AI-driven tools effectively and how AI can enhance their work. Provide training sessions that cover both technical aspects and strategic applications.

Monitor, Evaluate, and Adjust: Regularly monitor the performance of AI-driven workflows, and adjust as needed to address any new inefficiencies or bottlenecks. Continuous improvement ensures the technology remains relevant and effective over time.

7. Challenges in AI-Driven Workflow Optimization

While AI-driven workflow optimization offers numerous benefits, some challenges may arise during implementation:

Data Security and Privacy: As AI-driven systems process large amounts of sensitive procurement data, ensuring data security and compliance with privacy regulations is critical.

Change Management: Procurement teams may initially resist AI-driven workflow changes, especially if they feel their roles are being automated. Clear communication and engagement throughout the implementation process can help alleviate resistance.

Cost and Resource Allocation: Implementing AI can require significant resources, especially for organizations without existing AI infrastructure. Conducting a cost-benefit analysis helps ensure that the investment in AI is justified.

Dependency on Data Quality: AI algorithms are only as effective as the data they process. Poor data quality can result in inaccurate predictions and workflow issues. Investing in data governance and quality control measures is essential to maximize AI effectiveness.

8. Future Trends in AI-Driven Workflow Optimization

The future of AI-driven workflow optimization in procurement will be characterized by deeper integrations, greater adaptability, and expanded functionality. Emerging trends include:

Hyper-Automation: Combining AI, machine learning, and RPA to automate not only individual tasks but entire procurement processes, enabling seamless end-to-end workflow automation.

Adaptive AI: AI systems are expected to become more adaptive, learning from user behavior and adjusting workflows dynamically to optimize efficiency.

Enhanced Predictive Capabilities: Advanced predictive analytics will enable procurement teams to anticipate and prepare for various scenarios, such as supply chain disruptions, supplier risks, and demand fluctuations, with higher accuracy.

AI-driven workflow optimization has the power to reshape procurement, making it faster, more accurate, and more strategic. By focusing on AI tools that streamline key processes, procurement teams can create workflows that respond dynamically to business needs, support better decision-making, and add long-term value. With thoughtful implementation, organizations can harness AI to transform their procurement workflows and enhance the overall impact of procurement on organizational success.

Chapter 16: Streamlining Supplier Relationship Management with AI

Supplier relationship management (SRM) is a critical element of procurement that involves building, sustaining, and optimizing interactions with suppliers to foster collaboration, trust, and mutual benefits. Traditional SRM requires consistent communication, rigorous performance tracking, and relationship-building activities, which can be time-consuming and prone to inconsistencies. As procurement functions become more complex, Artificial Intelligence (AI) offers powerful solutions to streamline SRM processes, enhance communication, improve performance tracking, and strengthen supplier relationships.

This chapter explores how AI-driven tools are transforming SRM, offering procurement teams more efficient ways to manage supplier relationships, ensure quality, and collaborate effectively.

1. AI in Supplier Relationship Management: An Overview

AI-driven SRM leverages data, automation, and predictive analytics to enhance supplier interactions. While traditional SRM methods relied heavily on manual processes, email communication, and periodic performance reviews, AI allows procurement teams to interact with suppliers more seamlessly and make data-driven decisions.

AI transforms SRM through:

Automated Communication: AI-powered systems can send automated notifications, reminders, and updates, ensuring suppliers receive timely and relevant information.

Performance Analytics: Machine learning (ML) models analyze supplier performance over time, identifying trends and forecasting potential risks.

Predictive Insights: By analyzing past performance and market trends, AI helps procurement teams anticipate supplier challenges and proactively address issues.

2. Benefits of AI-Enhanced Supplier Relationship Management

AI provides numerous benefits for SRM, fundamentally changing the way procurement teams manage supplier partnerships:

Enhanced Communication: AI can automatically handle routine communication tasks, such as sharing forecasts, order changes, and compliance reminders. This ensures suppliers are always informed, and procurement teams spend less time on administrative tasks.

Improved Performance Tracking: AI-driven performance tracking gives real-time insights into supplier performance, quality metrics, and

133

delivery consistency. This enables procurement teams to respond quickly to issues, avoiding disruptions and ensuring high standards.

Proactive Issue Resolution: With predictive analytics, procurement teams can identify potential supply chain disruptions before they occur, allowing them to work with suppliers on preventive measures. This fosters a more collaborative relationship focused on problem-solving.

Data-Driven Relationship Building: AI tools provide comprehensive data on each supplier's strengths, areas for improvement, and contributions, helping procurement teams make informed decisions about which suppliers to prioritize and invest in long-term.

3. Key AI Applications in Supplier Relationship Management

AI can be applied in multiple SRM areas, with each application contributing to a more streamlined, effective supplier management process:

Supplier Performance Evaluation: AI-powered systems evaluate supplier performance based on several factors, such as on-time delivery rates, quality compliance, and responsiveness. Machine learning algorithms analyze historical data to score suppliers, track improvements, and highlight areas where additional support may be needed.

Automated Supplier Communication: Many AI tools include automated messaging capabilities, where procurement teams can set up notifications for order confirmations, status updates, and delivery schedules. Additionally, AI chatbots can assist with supplier queries, providing quick answers to standard questions and ensuring consistent communication.

Risk Assessment and Mitigation: AI-driven risk assessment tools analyze external factors, such as market trends, geopolitical risks, and supplier-specific issues, to provide risk scores for each supplier. These scores help procurement teams understand and prioritize potential vulnerabilities, reducing the impact of supply disruptions.

Predictive Supplier Performance: Machine learning models can predict supplier performance based on historical data, seasonal trends, and market shifts. For instance, if a supplier has consistently struggled with on-time delivery during peak seasons, AI can forecast similar performance issues and alert the procurement team to adjust order quantities or delivery timelines.

Supplier Development Planning: AI tools analyze data on supplier capabilities and areas for improvement, helping procurement teams design supplier development programs. By focusing on data-driven development, procurement teams can support suppliers in achieving higher standards, ultimately benefiting the organization.

4. Real-World Examples of AI in Supplier Relationship Management

Several organizations have successfully integrated AI to improve their supplier relationships, streamline communication, and enhance performance tracking:

Automated Communication at a Global Electronics Manufacturer: A multinational electronics manufacturer implemented AI-powered chatbots and automated notifications for supplier communication. By reducing manual messaging, the company decreased response times by 40%, enabling faster resolutions for order changes and delivery issues.

Predictive Analytics in Supplier Risk Management for a Pharmaceutical Company: A pharmaceutical company used AI-driven risk assessment tools to monitor global suppliers. Predictive analytics helped the company identify early signs of supply chain disruption due to geopolitical instability and adjust sourcing strategies to avoid shortages.

Data-Driven Supplier Development at a Retail Chain: A retail chain utilized AI analytics to evaluate supplier performance and design tailored development plans. The insights from AI allowed them to focus on specific areas, such as improving lead times and quality standards, leading to a 15% increase in supplier performance within six months.

5. Implementing AI for Supplier Relationship Management

Successful AI implementation for SRM requires planning, clear objectives, and stakeholder engagement. Here are the essential steps to consider:

Define SRM Goals and KPIs: Identify what you want to achieve with AI-driven SRM, such as reducing lead times, improving quality standards, or strengthening communication channels. Establish KPIs that will allow you to measure progress and outcomes.

Choose Appropriate AI Tools: Select AI tools that cater to your specific SRM needs. Consider factors like automation capabilities, real-time analytics, and ease of integration with your existing systems. Examples include AI-enabled SRM platforms, chatbots, and predictive analytics software.

Train Procurement Teams and Suppliers: Ensure procurement staff understand how to use AI tools effectively. Training sessions should focus on both technical skills and the strategic impact of AI-driven SRM. It may also be helpful to offer onboarding and support for suppliers who will interact with AI-enabled systems.

Monitor and Adjust: Continuously monitor the performance of AI-driven SRM tools, and make adjustments based on real-time feedback. This ensures that the AI system remains effective, and the organization maximizes the benefits of automation and predictive insights.

Encourage Supplier Engagement: Build a collaborative environment where suppliers understand the benefits of AI-driven SRM. Encourage them to share relevant data, follow best practices, and provide feedback on the AI-enabled system.

6. Challenges and Considerations in AI-Driven SRM

While AI-driven SRM provides numerous benefits, implementing it effectively involves overcoming a few challenges:

Data Privacy and Security: Supplier data may contain sensitive information. Organizations must prioritize data security, ensuring compliance with regulations like GDPR and implementing strong cybersecurity measures to protect supplier data.

Supplier Readiness and Cooperation: Not all suppliers may be ready to work with AI-driven systems. Smaller suppliers, in particular, may lack the technological infrastructure to fully integrate with AI tools, necessitating additional support and flexibility.

Change Management: Introducing AI can require a shift in how procurement teams interact with suppliers. Resistance to change can be mitigated by highlighting the benefits of AI for both suppliers and the organization, and by involving stakeholders throughout the implementation process.

Cost and ROI: Implementing AI in SRM may require a significant investment. Conducting a cost-benefit analysis helps ensure the financial resources are justified and allows the organization to track return on investment over time.

7. Future Trends in AI-Driven Supplier Relationship Management

As technology advances, several future trends are likely to shape AI-driven SRM:

Enhanced Predictive Capabilities: Future AI systems will incorporate even more sophisticated predictive analytics, helping procurement teams anticipate issues further in advance and respond proactively to changing supplier conditions.

Sentiment Analysis in Supplier Communication: Using natural language processing (NLP), AI tools will be able to assess the sentiment in supplier communications, providing insight into relationship health and allowing procurement teams to address concerns before they escalate.

Blockchain and AI Integration for Trust and Transparency: The integration of AI with blockchain technology is expected to enhance trust and transparency in supplier relationships. Blockchain's decentralized ledger will enable secure data sharing, while AI-driven insights provide real-time visibility into supplier performance and compliance.

Self-Learning SRM Systems: AI systems are evolving to be more adaptive, learning from interactions with suppliers and continuously improving communication patterns, performance evaluation criteria, and risk assessment capabilities.

AI-driven SRM represents a transformative approach to managing supplier relationships, providing procurement teams with powerful tools for streamlining processes, improving communication, and enhancing performance tracking. With thoughtful implementation and a focus on data-driven decision-making, organizations can leverage AI to build stronger, more resilient supplier partnerships that drive long-term value and strategic advantage. As AI technology continues to evolve, procurement teams will have even greater capabilities to foster supplier relationships that are collaborative, transparent, and equipped to adapt to future demands.

Part 5: AI-Powered Procurement Analytics

Chapter 17: Advanced Data Analytics in Procurement

In the modern procurement landscape, data analytics has emerged as a crucial tool for making informed decisions. By harnessing large volumes of data, procurement teams gain insights that guide strategic decisions, from supplier selection and contract negotiation to cost control and risk management. Traditional analytics approaches, however, often fall short when dealing with complex data sets or real-time demands. AI-powered analytics elevates this capability, enabling procurement professionals to make data-driven decisions faster, with greater accuracy, and on a larger scale.

This chapter delves into how advanced AI-driven data analytics is transforming procurement, providing procurement teams with a competitive edge in today's dynamic market.

1. The Evolution of Data Analytics in Procurement

Traditional data analytics in procurement primarily involved historical data analysis, trend identification, and reporting. While these insights were valuable, the approach was reactive, often based on past performance with limited predictive power. Additionally, manual data analysis could be time-consuming, susceptible to human error, and limited in scope.

With the rise of big data, AI-driven analytics tools have advanced significantly. AI can process large datasets from multiple sources, identify patterns, and deliver actionable insights in real time. Unlike traditional methods, AI-powered analytics not only interprets historical data but also predicts future trends, offering procurement teams a proactive decision-making tool.

2. The Role of AI in Advanced Procurement Analytics

AI's application in procurement analytics spans a variety of areas, enhancing procurement's strategic role within organizations:

Data Aggregation: AI tools can gather and unify data from diverse sources such as internal ERP systems, market reports, supplier databases, and news feeds. This consolidated data provides a holistic view of procurement and supply chain dynamics, leading to more comprehensive analyses.

Pattern Recognition: Machine learning (ML) algorithms are highly effective in recognizing patterns in data that may not be immediately apparent. These patterns help procurement teams identify trends and outliers, enabling them to make preemptive decisions and mitigate risks.

Real-Time Insights: AI tools can provide continuous, real-time insights by analyzing data instantly as it becomes available. This allows procurement teams to respond immediately to changes, from shifts in supplier performance to fluctuations in market pricing, improving responsiveness and adaptability.

Predictive Analytics: AI algorithms analyze historical data to forecast future events such as demand fluctuations, supplier performance changes, and price trends. Predictive analytics enables procurement teams to make forward-looking decisions, improve planning, and reduce potential disruptions.

Prescriptive Analytics: In addition to predicting outcomes, AI-driven prescriptive analytics tools can recommend specific actions based on data. For example, prescriptive analytics might suggest reordering from a supplier based on anticipated lead times and demand forecasts.

3. Key Applications of AI-Driven Analytics in Procurement

AI-powered data analytics can be applied to various facets of procurement, each contributing to data-driven decision-making:

Spend Analysis: AI tools classify and analyze spending data across departments, categories, and suppliers. This comprehensive analysis helps procurement teams identify cost-saving opportunities, optimize budgets, and consolidate suppliers to negotiate better rates.

Supplier Performance Analytics: AI-driven analytics track supplier performance over time by monitoring factors like delivery times, quality rates, and compliance. These insights help procurement teams identify reliable suppliers, predict potential issues, and make informed decisions about supplier relationships.

Market Intelligence and Pricing Analysis: AI can monitor market trends, analyze price fluctuations, and assess supply-demand dynamics, providing procurement teams with accurate pricing information. This helps them negotiate more favorable contracts and minimize costs when prices are projected to rise.

Demand Forecasting: AI-based demand forecasting uses historical sales data, seasonal trends, and external market conditions to predict future demand. This enables procurement teams to maintain optimal inventory levels, reduce stockouts, and avoid overstocking.

Risk Assessment and Mitigation: AI-driven risk analytics evaluate risk factors associated with suppliers, markets, and geopolitical conditions. Predictive risk assessment tools provide early warnings of potential disruptions, enabling procurement teams to develop contingency plans and minimize impact.

Contract Compliance and Optimization: AI tools can analyze contract terms and conditions, monitor compliance, and track contract utilization. This ensures that procurement teams are fully utilizing negotiated terms, maximizing value, and maintaining compliance.

144

4. Benefits of AI-Powered Analytics in Procurement

AI-powered analytics deliver significant advantages that enhance procurement efficiency, cost-effectiveness, and decision-making quality:

Increased Efficiency: Automation of data collection, classification, and analysis saves time for procurement teams, allowing them to focus on strategic activities rather than manual data handling.

Cost Savings: By identifying spending patterns and potential cost-saving opportunities, AI-driven analytics enable procurement teams to make more economical choices, negotiate better deals, and reduce waste.

Enhanced Accuracy: AI reduces the risk of human error in data analysis, providing procurement teams with more reliable insights that lead to better decisions.

Faster Decision-Making: With real-time data analysis, procurement teams can make timely decisions, responding to changes in supplier performance, demand, or market conditions without delay.

Informed Strategic Planning: Predictive analytics and trend forecasting provide procurement leaders with insights that aid in long-term planning, supporting initiatives such as supplier diversification, category management, and sustainability goals.

5. Real-World Applications of AI Analytics in Procurement

Many companies across various industries have successfully integrated AI-powered analytics to optimize their procurement processes:

145

Spend Optimization at a Consumer Goods Company: A global consumer goods company used AI-driven spend analytics to consolidate supplier contracts and identify high-spending areas across its branches. This led to a 12% reduction in procurement costs and a more streamlined supplier base.

Supplier Risk Assessment in a Pharmaceutical Company: A large pharmaceutical firm employed AI-based risk analytics to evaluate supplier reliability. By analyzing historical performance data and external risk factors, the company predicted potential disruptions and diversified its supplier portfolio, reducing dependency on high-risk suppliers.

Price Forecasting in a Manufacturing Firm: A manufacturing company used AI-powered market intelligence tools to analyze raw material pricing trends. With these insights, procurement teams negotiated fixed pricing contracts ahead of anticipated price increases, saving 15% in raw material costs over the next fiscal year.

6. Implementing AI Analytics in Procurement

To successfully implement AI-powered analytics in procurement, organizations should follow a few key steps:

Define Clear Objectives: Establish what you aim to achieve with AI analytics, such as reducing procurement costs, improving supplier quality, or mitigating risks. Defining clear objectives helps ensure the analytics approach aligns with business goals.

Choose the Right Tools and Technology: Select AI tools that cater to the specific needs of procurement. These tools may include spend analysis software, predictive analytics platforms, and supplier performance monitoring systems.

Ensure Data Quality and Integration: AI tools require high-quality, integrated data for optimal performance. Work with IT and data teams to clean, organize, and integrate procurement data from various sources, such as ERP systems, supplier portals, and market intelligence databases.

Train Procurement Teams: AI tools can be complex, so providing training for procurement staff is essential. Training should cover data interpretation, software usage, and integrating insights into decision-making processes.

Monitor and Evaluate Outcomes: Continuously track the performance of AI analytics to measure outcomes against objectives. Use insights from this evaluation to adjust your approach and maximize the benefits of AI in procurement analytics.

7. Challenges in AI-Driven Procurement Analytics

Despite its benefits, implementing AI-powered analytics in procurement comes with several challenges:

Data Privacy and Security: With the increased amount of data used for analysis, ensuring data privacy and security is critical. Organizations must implement robust cybersecurity measures and comply with regulations like GDPR.

147

Quality and Accessibility of Data: AI-driven analytics depend on high-quality data. Inconsistent or incomplete data can hinder analytics accuracy and limit the effectiveness of insights.

Complexity and Costs of Implementation: Setting up AI-powered analytics can require significant investments in software, training, and data integration. Organizations should perform a cost-benefit analysis to assess the value of AI analytics against its implementation costs.

Resistance to Change: Procurement teams may be reluctant to shift from traditional methods to AI-driven analytics. Change management efforts, including training and highlighting AI's benefits, can help overcome resistance.

8. Future Trends in AI-Powered Procurement Analytics

The future of AI-driven procurement analytics promises further advancements in data analysis and decision-making:

AI-Augmented Decision Support: Emerging AI technologies will provide more sophisticated decision support, enabling procurement teams to make complex, multi-faceted decisions with greater confidence.

Natural Language Processing for Unstructured Data: NLP will allow AI to analyze unstructured data from supplier communications, market news, and social media, adding valuable context to procurement analytics.

Blockchain for Data Integrity: The integration of blockchain technology with AI analytics will provide procurement teams with data that is tamper-proof and more reliable, enhancing the transparency and trustworthiness of insights.

Self-Learning Analytics Systems: Future AI analytics platforms will have self-learning capabilities, enabling them to adapt to changes in procurement needs and refine insights continuously.

AI-powered analytics is transforming procurement by providing teams with a powerful tool for data-driven decision-making. With the ability to analyze complex data sets in real-time, identify trends, and predict outcomes, AI analytics empowers procurement teams to make faster, more accurate, and more strategic decisions. As the technology evolves, its role in procurement will expand, further cementing data analytics as a cornerstone of modern procurement strategy.

Chapter 18: Real-Time Insights and Dynamic Reporting

In today's fast-paced business environment, real-time information is vital for making responsive and well-informed procurement decisions. Real-time insights and dynamic reporting enable procurement teams to act quickly and proactively in response to changing conditions. Traditional reporting methods, which rely on historical data and static reports, often fall short when immediate action is required. AI technology is redefining reporting and insights generation in procurement, providing continuous, up-to-date information that enhances decision-making at every level.

In this chapter, we'll explore how AI empowers procurement professionals to leverage real-time data and dynamic reporting, driving operational efficiency, cost savings, and greater visibility across the supply chain.

1. The Shift to Real-Time Information in Procurement

Historically, procurement reporting relied on data that was processed and analyzed periodically, often resulting in time lags between data collection and action. Monthly or quarterly reports provided useful insights but were often outdated by the time they reached decision-makers, limiting responsiveness and agility. Today, procurement operates in a dynamic environment with rapid changes in supply and demand, fluctuating prices, and shifting supplier performance levels. Real-time insights and dynamic reporting address these challenges by providing continuous, actionable information that enables procurement teams to respond immediately to emerging trends and disruptions.

2. How AI Enables Real-Time Insights

AI-driven platforms generate real-time insights by continuously gathering, processing, and analyzing data from multiple sources. Key enablers of AI-powered real-time insights include:

Data Aggregation and Integration: AI tools consolidate data from various sources, including ERP systems, supplier portals, market intelligence platforms, and external news sources. This integration provides a comprehensive view of procurement activities and market conditions in a single interface.

Automated Data Processing: Machine learning algorithms automate the processing and analysis of data as soon as it's collected, enabling instant transformation of raw data into actionable insights.

Natural Language Processing (NLP): NLP allows AI to understand unstructured data, such as supplier communications or news articles, transforming this information into valuable insights that can complement structured data sources.

Predictive and Prescriptive Analytics: Real-time AI-driven insights aren't just descriptive—they also offer predictive and prescriptive analytics. AI algorithms can identify potential risks, forecast demand trends, and recommend proactive actions, allowing procurement teams to stay ahead of potential disruptions.

3. Applications of Real-Time Insights in Procurement

AI-driven real-time insights and dynamic reporting can transform several areas within procurement, delivering greater responsiveness and efficiency:

Supplier Monitoring and Risk Management: Real-time insights allow procurement teams to monitor supplier performance continuously. By analyzing data on lead times, quality metrics, and financial stability, AI can alert procurement teams to potential issues, such as a supplier's declining performance or financial instability, enabling proactive measures to mitigate risks.

Market Price Fluctuations: In volatile markets, real-time insights into price changes can help procurement professionals make timely purchasing decisions. For instance, if the price of a critical material spikes due to supply chain disruptions, real-time price monitoring enables procurement teams to take action quickly, securing alternative sources or adjusting purchasing quantities.

Inventory and Demand Adjustments: AI-powered demand forecasting can provide real-time insights into shifts in demand, helping procurement teams manage inventory more effectively. For example, if demand is expected to surge due to seasonal trends or unexpected events, procurement teams can adjust order quantities to ensure adequate stock levels.

Spend Analysis and Budget Management: Real-time spend insights allow procurement teams to track budgets continuously, reducing the risk of overspending and identifying cost-saving opportunities immediately. Dynamic reporting can show spending patterns across categories, departments, or time periods, empowering procurement to make quick adjustments when necessary.

Contract Compliance Monitoring: AI-based systems can monitor real-time contract compliance by analyzing purchase orders, invoices, and supplier performance data against contract terms. This helps procurement teams identify any deviations and take corrective action, maximizing contract value and reducing potential penalties.

4. Benefits of Real-Time Insights and Dynamic Reporting

Adopting real-time insights and dynamic reporting offers procurement teams a variety of advantages, particularly in today's increasingly complex supply chain environment:

Enhanced Responsiveness: With real-time data, procurement teams can respond immediately to changes in supplier performance, market conditions, or internal demand shifts. This responsiveness reduces lead times, minimizes risks, and helps maintain smooth operations even under unexpected conditions.

153

Greater Agility: Dynamic reporting enables procurement to make quick decisions based on the latest data. Agility in decision-making allows companies to adapt their strategies to market changes, stay ahead of competitors, and seize opportunities as they arise.

Increased Cost Control: Real-time spend analysis helps procurement teams manage budgets effectively, allowing for immediate identification of any overspending or inefficiencies. By acting quickly on spending insights, procurement can optimize costs and improve financial performance.

Improved Supplier Relationships: Continuous monitoring and real-time feedback can foster stronger relationships with suppliers. By identifying issues as soon as they arise, procurement teams can work collaboratively with suppliers to address problems, enhancing trust and long-term partnerships.

Better Risk Mitigation: Real-time risk monitoring provides early warnings about potential disruptions, enabling procurement teams to take preemptive actions, such as finding alternative suppliers or adjusting inventory levels, to reduce the impact of potential risks.

5. Examples of Real-Time Insights and Dynamic Reporting in Practice

Numerous companies across industries have integrated real-time insights and dynamic reporting into their procurement functions with measurable results:

Automobile Manufacturer: A global automobile manufacturer used real-time insights to monitor supplier quality. By analyzing data on defect rates and delivery timelines, the company was able to flag potential quality issues early, enabling collaboration with suppliers to improve processes and maintain production schedules.

Retailer Demand Forecasting: A large retail chain implemented real-time demand forecasting, using AI to track and predict purchasing trends. When customer demand spiked unexpectedly, procurement was able to adjust its orders in real time, avoiding stockouts and meeting customer demand seamlessly.

Pharmaceutical Company Risk Management: A pharmaceutical company leveraged real-time supplier risk analytics to monitor supplier performance and compliance. When one supplier showed signs of financial instability, the procurement team received alerts and quickly sourced an alternative supplier, avoiding potential disruptions to production.

6. Implementing Real-Time Insights in Procurement

To effectively implement real-time insights and dynamic reporting, procurement teams should focus on several key factors:

Adopt Advanced Analytics Tools: Select analytics tools and AI platforms that provide real-time data processing and reporting capabilities. The right tools will integrate seamlessly with existing systems and provide an easy-to-navigate dashboard for monitoring insights.

Integrate Data Sources: Real-time insights rely on data from diverse sources, so it's essential to integrate data across ERP systems, supplier portals, and external data feeds. This ensures that insights are comprehensive and reliable.

Prioritize Data Quality: The accuracy of real-time insights depends on the quality of the data being analyzed. Ensure that all data sources are updated regularly and validated for accuracy and consistency.

Train Procurement Teams: Training is essential to help procurement professionals understand how to interpret real-time data and act on insights effectively. Training should also cover any new software or AI tools used to generate real-time insights.

Establish Real-Time Monitoring Metrics: Define clear KPIs and metrics for monitoring real-time procurement activities. Common metrics might include supplier lead times, contract compliance rates, budget adherence, and demand fluctuation levels.

7. Challenges of Real-Time Insights and Dynamic Reporting

Implementing real-time insights in procurement does present challenges, including:

Data Overload: Real-time data can sometimes lead to information overload, with teams receiving more data than they can process effectively. Setting filters and prioritizing high-impact alerts can help manage data volume.

Integration Complexity: Integrating real-time data from multiple sources, such as external market feeds and internal ERP systems, can be complex and time-consuming. A well-structured data integration strategy and investment in compatible tools are essential.

Change Management: Shifting from periodic to real-time reporting requires a cultural shift within procurement teams. Change management strategies, including training and communication of benefits, can help ease this transition.

Cybersecurity Risks: Real-time data processing requires robust cybersecurity measures to protect sensitive procurement data from potential breaches.

8. The Future of Real-Time Insights in Procurement

The future of procurement will increasingly rely on real-time insights as AI technology and data integration capabilities continue to advance. Trends that will shape the future include:

Augmented Reality (AR) for Dynamic Reporting: Procurement teams may use AR to visualize real-time data in immersive formats, such as interactive dashboards displayed on smart glasses, enhancing the speed and accuracy of decision-making.

Predictive Analytics with IoT Data: As the Internet of Things (IoT) expands, IoT-generated data on everything from shipment tracking to equipment conditions can be analyzed in real time to provide deeper insights into supply chain dynamics.

Blockchain for Data Integrity: Blockchain technology will enhance data integrity, ensuring that real-time procurement insights are based on verifiable and tamper-proof data, improving trust in insights generated.

Self-Optimizing Analytics Systems: Future AI systems will be self-learning, automatically refining data analysis models based on changing procurement needs, enhancing the relevance and accuracy of real-time insights continuously.

AI-powered real-time insights and dynamic reporting represent a transformative shift in procurement, enabling a proactive, agile approach to decision-making. With instant access to data on supplier performance, spending, and market trends, procurement teams are better equipped to navigate the complexities of today's global supply chain. By adopting these technologies, organizations can improve operational efficiency, foster stronger supplier relationships, and ultimately gain a competitive advantage in the marketplace.

Chapter 19: Sentiment Analysis in Supplier Feedback

Effective supplier relationship management is central to a successful procurement strategy. While traditional methods for evaluating supplier performance focus on quantitative metrics such as delivery timelines, defect rates, and compliance, qualitative insights — such as supplier sentiment — are equally valuable but harder to capture. Sentiment analysis, a branch of natural language processing (NLP), enables procurement teams to gain a nuanced understanding of supplier performance and engagement by analyzing feedback, communications, and other textual data for sentiment, tone, and underlying attitudes.

In this chapter, we'll explore how sentiment analysis works, its applications in procurement, and its impact on supplier relationship management. By leveraging sentiment analysis, procurement teams can make more informed, relationship-oriented decisions that foster long-term collaboration and support the organization's strategic objectives.

1. The Value of Supplier Sentiment Analysis

Sentiment analysis goes beyond conventional metrics by evaluating subjective aspects of supplier interactions. Suppliers' attitudes, willingness to collaborate, and levels of satisfaction directly affect service quality and reliability, which can impact the entire supply chain. For example, suppliers who feel valued and supported are more likely to respond positively to urgent requests, offer competitive prices, or collaborate on product innovations. Conversely, suppliers who feel undervalued may deprioritize certain orders, or delay responses, affecting the organization's ability to meet customer demands.

By applying sentiment analysis to supplier communications, performance reviews, survey responses, and other feedback sources, procurement teams can:

Identify early signs of dissatisfaction: Detecting and addressing supplier issues early can prevent potential disruptions.

Enhance supplier collaboration: Positive supplier sentiment can indicate readiness to collaborate on innovative solutions, joint problem-solving, or long-term agreements.

Refine contract negotiations: Procurement teams can use sentiment insights to structure negotiations in ways that reinforce positive engagement.

Assess the effectiveness of procurement policies: Sentiment analysis helps determine if procurement practices support constructive supplier relationships.

2. How Sentiment Analysis Works in Supplier Feedback

Sentiment analysis in procurement involves using NLP algorithms to analyze text data from supplier communications and feedback, identifying positive, neutral, or negative sentiment. The analysis leverages several key NLP techniques:

Text Parsing and Tokenization: The text data is parsed and broken down into individual components (tokens), such as words and phrases, which are analyzed to determine meaning.

Part-of-Speech Tagging: Identifying the grammatical structure of sentences, such as nouns, verbs, and adjectives, helps the algorithm understand the context.

Sentiment Scoring: Words and phrases are matched against a lexicon of positive, neutral, and negative terms, with sentiment scores assigned to reflect the overall tone of each message.

Contextual Analysis: Advanced models consider context to avoid misinterpretations. For example, words like "demanding" can imply either a positive or negative sentiment based on the sentence's overall context.

AI algorithms can also be trained on historical procurement data to recognize industry-specific terms and context, improving accuracy and relevance in supplier sentiment analysis.

3. Key Applications of Sentiment Analysis in Procurement

Sentiment analysis provides procurement teams with real-time, actionable insights across various areas of supplier management, including:

Supplier Performance Assessment: By analyzing written feedback and communications, procurement teams can supplement quantitative metrics with qualitative data that reflects supplier morale and satisfaction. For instance, if a supplier frequently expresses frustration in emails or feedback forms, it may signal underlying issues with order volume, timelines, or payment terms.

Supplier Selection and Vetting: During the supplier selection phase, sentiment analysis can help assess a supplier's commitment and attitude toward potential partnerships. Positive sentiment in early communications may indicate a high level of engagement, while negative sentiment could suggest potential friction.

Contract Negotiation and Renewal: Understanding a supplier's sentiment can inform negotiation strategies, helping procurement teams structure terms that promote positive engagement. If sentiment analysis reveals high satisfaction, it may be an opportune time to negotiate for cost savings or extended terms; conversely, negative sentiment may indicate the need for contract adjustments to maintain the relationship.

Monitoring Supplier Relationships: Continuous monitoring of sentiment across interactions with suppliers provides a pulse check on supplier relationships, allowing teams to address any issues proactively.

Risk Management: Negative sentiment trends in supplier feedback may point to risks, such as a supplier's reduced commitment, financial instability, or other performance issues. Early identification of these risks enables procurement teams to take preemptive action, mitigating potential disruptions.

4. Benefits of Sentiment Analysis in Supplier Management

Implementing sentiment analysis in procurement offers several advantages that contribute to better supplier relationship management and overall supply chain performance:

Enhanced Supplier Communication: Procurement teams gain a deeper understanding of suppliers' perspectives, fostering more empathetic and responsive communication. This can improve supplier loyalty, which is especially beneficial during periods of high demand or supply chain disruptions.

Improved Supplier Retention: Positive relationships are essential for long-term partnerships. By proactively addressing negative sentiment, procurement can prevent supplier churn, retaining reliable suppliers who understand the organization's requirements and quality standards.

Increased Negotiation Leverage: Understanding supplier sentiment offers strategic insights that can be used to strengthen procurement's negotiating position. Procurement teams can capitalize on positive sentiment to secure favorable terms and address negative sentiment to alleviate supplier concerns.

Strengthened Supplier Collaboration: Sentiment analysis identifies suppliers who are enthusiastic and willing to collaborate on joint ventures or product improvements, fostering innovation within the supply chain.

Early Risk Detection: Detecting negative sentiment allows for early risk mitigation, helping to avoid costly disruptions. By acting on sentiment data, procurement teams can engage with suppliers to resolve grievances before they escalate into operational issues.

5. Implementing Sentiment Analysis in Procurement Processes

To successfully implement sentiment analysis in procurement, teams should follow a strategic approach that includes selecting the right technology, integrating data sources, and fostering a culture of collaboration and transparency:

Select Suitable NLP Tools: Choose sentiment analysis tools that support industry-specific language processing and can be customized to your organization's needs. Many AI platforms offer sentiment analysis capabilities that can be tailored to procurement, analyzing large volumes of data efficiently.

Integrate Diverse Data Sources: Sentiment analysis is most effective when applied to a variety of data sources, including email correspondence, survey responses, supplier review documents, and social media mentions. By aggregating data from these sources, procurement teams gain a comprehensive view of supplier sentiment.

Set Clear Sentiment Metrics: Establish metrics that define sentiment trends, such as positive, neutral, or negative sentiment thresholds. These metrics enable procurement teams to monitor sentiment consistently and make data-driven decisions.

Train Procurement Teams on Interpretation: Procurement professionals should understand how to interpret sentiment scores and contextualize insights. Training helps teams apply sentiment data effectively, ensuring that insights lead to actionable outcomes.

Use Sentiment Insights in Decision-Making: Integrate sentiment analysis insights into routine procurement decisions, such as supplier performance reviews, contract renewals, and risk assessments.

Embedding sentiment data in decision-making ensures a balanced approach that considers both quantitative and qualitative information.

6. Potential Challenges and Limitations

While sentiment analysis offers substantial benefits, procurement teams should be mindful of the potential challenges:

Contextual Nuances: Sentiment analysis may struggle with ambiguous language or industry-specific jargon. Phrases that convey subtle meanings may be misinterpreted, leading to inaccurate sentiment scores.

Data Privacy and Compliance: Analyzing supplier communications for sentiment requires adherence to data privacy regulations and may necessitate supplier consent. Procurement teams should establish clear policies for ethical data handling.

Bias in Sentiment Models: Sentiment analysis algorithms may reflect biases present in the data or the model's training set. Regular model evaluations are essential to ensure fair and accurate sentiment assessments.

Limited Insight in Small Datasets: If supplier interactions are limited or infrequent, sentiment analysis may not provide meaningful insights. In such cases, procurement teams should supplement sentiment data with other qualitative insights gathered through direct supplier conversations or site visits.

7. Future Trends in Sentiment Analysis for Procurement

Advancements in AI and NLP are continually enhancing sentiment analysis, and future developments are expected to provide even more precise insights for procurement. Emerging trends include:

Multilingual Sentiment Analysis: As global supply chains expand, multilingual sentiment analysis will allow procurement teams to evaluate feedback from suppliers worldwide, regardless of language. Advanced NLP models are increasingly capable of analyzing sentiment in multiple languages, improving global supplier management.

Emotion Detection: Beyond basic sentiment, AI is advancing toward detecting specific emotions such as frustration, enthusiasm, or uncertainty. Emotion detection offers a more nuanced understanding of supplier attitudes and can guide more personalized responses.

Voice Sentiment Analysis: Some AI models are beginning to analyze sentiment in spoken communication, such as phone calls or virtual meetings. Voice sentiment analysis would add another dimension to supplier relationship management, enabling real-time sentiment tracking during conversations.

Automated Sentiment Action Triggers: AI-based systems may soon automate certain responses based on sentiment analysis. For instance, a consistently negative sentiment trend could trigger alerts for procurement teams to review the supplier relationship, or a highly positive sentiment could suggest exploring collaborative initiatives.

Sentiment analysis offers procurement teams a powerful tool for understanding and managing supplier relationships. By incorporating this qualitative data into procurement processes, organizations can create more responsive, relationship-oriented strategies that enhance supplier satisfaction, mitigate risks, and support operational goals. In an era where strong supplier relationships are increasingly crucial for supply chain resilience, sentiment analysis provides the insights necessary to build and sustain productive partnerships.

Part 6: Implementation and Integration of AI in Procurement

Chapter 20: Building the AI-Ready Procurement Function

Implementing AI in procurement isn't simply a matter of acquiring technology. For AI to provide meaningful insights and deliver optimal results, procurement functions must undergo a strategic transformation that prepares them for AI integration. This preparation involves establishing an AI-ready culture, structuring data processes, upskilling teams, and building an ecosystem that integrates seamlessly with advanced technologies.

In this chapter, we'll examine the essential steps for building an AI-ready procurement function, focusing on team preparation, system adjustments, data management, and creating an adaptable, technology-friendly environment.

1. Defining the AI Vision for Procurement

Before beginning the implementation process, organizations must establish a clear vision for how AI will transform their procurement function. This includes identifying specific objectives for AI usage, such as improving decision-making accuracy, enhancing cost-efficiency, and creating real-time insights for better supplier management. A strong AI vision helps align procurement strategies with organizational goals and sets a foundation for selecting the right AI tools and processes.

Key Actions:

Establish Objectives: Outline specific areas where AI is expected to add value, such as supplier selection, spend analytics, or risk management.

Align with Business Goals: Ensure AI initiatives support the broader business objectives, enhancing efficiency, innovation, and competitive advantage.

Involve Stakeholders: Engage key stakeholders early to gain buy-in and refine the AI vision based on cross-functional insights.

2. Preparing Teams for AI Integration

AI in procurement requires teams to shift from traditional, manual processes to data-driven and automated decision-making. Preparing teams for this transition involves a combination of skills training, mindset shifts, and fostering collaboration between procurement and IT departments.

Key Steps:

Skill Development: Upskill teams with AI and data literacy, teaching them how to interpret AI outputs, work with algorithms, and leverage data for strategic decisions.

Mindset Shift: Encourage a culture of curiosity and openness to technology, where procurement professionals see AI as an enabler, not a threat to their roles.

Cross-Functional Collaboration: Foster collaboration between procurement and IT teams, ensuring both understand the requirements and limitations of AI. Regular cross-training sessions can be helpful to align these teams on common objectives.

Example of Key Skills to Develop:

Data Analysis: Equip procurement teams with basic data analysis skills, allowing them to understand and utilize AI-generated insights effectively.

Technical Literacy: Provide a foundational understanding of AI concepts, such as machine learning, natural language processing, and predictive analytics.

Problem-Solving Using AI: Enable teams to approach procurement challenges through AI-based solutions, integrating AI thinking into their strategic and operational decision-making.

3. Structuring and Cleansing Data for AI Use

High-quality data is the backbone of any successful AI implementation. AI algorithms need clean, consistent, and relevant data to produce reliable outputs. For procurement, this means that data on suppliers, contracts, transactions, and performance metrics should be carefully structured and regularly updated.

Data Preparation Strategies:

Data Cleansing: Remove or rectify incomplete, outdated, or duplicated data. AI models depend on accurate data for producing actionable insights.

Standardization: Implement standardized data formats across procurement systems to make integration easier. This involves ensuring all data fields follow consistent naming conventions and units of measurement.

Data Enrichment: Augment existing procurement data with third-party or industry data for more comprehensive insights. External data sources can add value, particularly for benchmarking or evaluating market conditions.

Data Governance Policies: Establish data governance policies that define data ownership, responsibilities, and security, ensuring data is managed and stored responsibly.

Example:

An organization planning to use AI for spend analytics needs clean and standardized data on spending across departments. By standardizing and cleaning this data, the procurement team can confidently use AI models to detect spending patterns, identify cost-saving opportunities, and make more accurate forecasts.

4. Selecting AI-Enabled Procurement Technologies

Once the procurement function is ready to support AI, it's time to select suitable AI tools that align with the organization's needs and AI vision. Different AI applications will require different capabilities, so it's important to evaluate tools based on their fit with organizational goals, ease of use, scalability, and integration capacity with existing systems.

Considerations When Selecting AI Tools:

Capabilities: Choose tools with the functionalities necessary for your key objectives, such as predictive analytics, supplier risk assessment, or spend optimization.

User-Friendly Interface: Tools with intuitive, user-friendly interfaces will make it easier for procurement teams to adopt and use AI features effectively.

Integration Potential: Opt for tools that can be integrated seamlessly with existing systems, such as ERP, CRM, or legacy procurement software, minimizing the learning curve.

Scalability: Select technologies that can scale with your organization's growth, allowing for expanded functionality or additional users over time.

Types of AI Tools for Procurement:

Supplier Risk Management Platforms: AI-based platforms analyze supplier data to detect potential risks, predict issues, and propose mitigation strategies.

Spend Analytics Software: Tools that leverage AI for detailed analysis of spend data, highlighting trends, cost-saving opportunities, and compliance gaps.

Contract Management Solutions: AI-powered solutions streamline contract analysis, using NLP to identify risk clauses, ensure compliance, and manage contract renewal timelines.

5. Building Data Infrastructure to Support AI Integration

A robust data infrastructure is necessary for AI in procurement to function effectively. This involves developing systems for data storage, processing, and analysis, with a strong focus on security, accessibility, and scalability.

Key Components of an AI-Ready Data Infrastructure:

Centralized Data Storage: Implement a centralized data repository where all procurement data is stored, ensuring consistent access for AI models. Cloud-based storage solutions are particularly effective for supporting real-time AI applications.

Data Security Measures: AI models require access to sensitive procurement and supplier information. Ensure that data storage solutions comply with industry standards for data security and privacy, including encryption and access control.

Real-Time Data Processing: Real-time data processing enables AI models to deliver up-to-date insights. For example, real-time data allows procurement teams to access instant spending updates, monitor contract compliance, or track supplier performance.

6. Testing and Piloting AI in Procurement

Before rolling out AI technologies organization-wide, it's essential to conduct pilot programs that test AI applications in controlled settings. Piloting helps identify any gaps in the AI model, data inaccuracies, or technical issues that could impact performance when scaled.

Steps to Effective AI Piloting:

Define Pilot Objectives: Establish clear objectives for what the pilot aims to achieve, such as improved demand forecasting accuracy, faster contract analysis, or enhanced supplier risk assessment.

Select Relevant Metrics: Choose metrics that align with pilot objectives, ensuring progress is measurable. For instance, time savings, forecast accuracy, or contract processing speed are valuable indicators of AI's effectiveness.

Evaluate and Refine: After the pilot phase, gather feedback, evaluate results, and refine AI processes as needed. Adjustments may include retraining AI models, optimizing data inputs, or addressing any identified gaps in user understanding.

Example Pilot Project:

A pilot project for implementing AI in spend analytics might begin with a limited department or region. By running this project in a controlled environment, procurement can evaluate how AI insights impact spending decisions, adjusting the model for broader application if successful.

7. Embedding AI-Driven Decision-Making in Procurement Processes

For AI to be effective in procurement, it needs to be embedded within standard processes and decision-making frameworks. This integration ensures that AI insights are actively utilized rather than treated as supplementary data.

Embedding AI in Procurement Decisions:

Integrate AI Insights in Daily Operations: Ensure that AI outputs are readily available to procurement professionals during decision-making processes. For instance, supplier risk scores can be reviewed before approving contracts, and demand forecasts can be used in inventory planning.

Encourage Data-Driven Culture: Promote a culture where decisions are based on data insights, and AI tools are trusted as part of the procurement team's toolkit. Regular training and showcasing AI success stories can reinforce this culture.

Review and Adjust AI Models Regularly: AI models need regular reviews to stay aligned with changing procurement goals or market conditions. This involves periodically retraining models, updating data inputs, and refining algorithms based on feedback from procurement teams.

8. Monitoring Performance and Continuous Improvement

Once AI is integrated into procurement, ongoing performance monitoring is critical to ensure it meets evolving needs and delivers the intended value. Procurement teams should establish a continuous improvement cycle where AI tools and processes are regularly assessed and optimized.

Key Aspects of Performance Monitoring:

Define Key Performance Indicators (KPIs): Establish KPIs relevant to AI integration, such as cost savings, process efficiency, and user satisfaction.

Collect Feedback: Gather feedback from procurement teams and other stakeholders to identify areas for improvement and refine AI applications as needed.

Update AI Models: AI models should be updated based on performance feedback and data changes, ensuring they remain accurate and valuable to procurement teams.

Building an AI-ready procurement function is a transformative process that requires a strategic approach to team preparation, data management, and technology integration. By fostering an AI-friendly culture, developing robust data infrastructures, and embedding AI-driven decision-making into procurement processes, organizations can unlock the full potential of AI to drive efficiency, agility, and strategic value within procurement.

This preparation is critical for a successful AI rollout and forms the foundation for future advancements in procurement technology, empowering procurement teams to make informed, data-driven decisions and improve supplier relationships. As AI continues to evolve, procurement functions that embrace this transformation will be better positioned to stay competitive and adaptive in a rapidly changing market.

Chapter 21: Selecting and Implementing AI Solutions

As AI continues to reshape procurement, selecting the right AI tools and implementing them effectively has become essential for organizations aiming to enhance operational efficiency, cost savings, and strategic capabilities. However, the selection and deployment process can be complex, given the multitude of AI solutions available, each with its unique features, data requirements, and potential benefits.

This chapter provides a roadmap for procurement leaders on how to choose, evaluate, and integrate AI solutions tailored to their specific needs. It covers essential selection criteria, key implementation steps, and strategies for aligning AI tools with overall procurement goals.

1. Understanding Procurement's AI Needs and Objectives

The selection process for AI solutions should begin with a thorough assessment of the procurement department's goals, challenges, and anticipated benefits. Clearly defined objectives help narrow down the tools that will be most effective and provide the structure necessary for evaluating performance later on.

Defining Objectives for AI Integration:

Cost Optimization: AI tools can identify savings opportunities by analyzing spend data, suggesting alternate suppliers, or predicting demand more accurately.

Process Automation: Reducing manual tasks like purchase order creation, invoice processing, and data entry through AI-driven automation.

Risk Management: Identifying supplier-related risks and other vulnerabilities through AI-powered risk analysis tools.

Enhanced Supplier Management: Utilizing AI to assess supplier performance and ensure alignment with the organization's quality and ethical standards.

Example Goal Setting:

A company focusing on risk reduction may prioritize AI solutions that offer predictive analytics for supplier risk assessment. Conversely, an organization aiming to streamline workflows might seek tools that emphasize automation for procurement tasks.

2. Evaluating Key Features and Capabilities of AI Solutions

Procurement teams must review AI solutions based on their specific features and capabilities. This assessment ensures that the selected tools offer functionalities that align with procurement objectives while also considering the organization's technical environment and team expertise.

Core Capabilities to Consider:

Data Analytics and Insights: Robust analytics capabilities to analyze spend, identify trends, and generate actionable insights.

Automation Potential: The ability to automate routine tasks such as contract reviews, compliance checks, and data entry to save time and reduce errors.

Predictive Analytics: Advanced forecasting to anticipate demand, supplier behavior, and pricing trends.

Natural Language Processing (NLP): NLP capabilities to analyze text-heavy documents like contracts, supplier feedback, and communication records.

Real-Time Reporting: Dynamic reporting features that provide up-to-date insights to support fast, data-driven decisions.

Feature Assessment Example:

For a procurement team focused on spend analytics, an AI tool with strong data analytics capabilities and customizable reporting might be prioritized over a solution focused on automation or NLP.

3. Assessing Vendor Compatibility and Support

Once the desired features are identified, the next step involves evaluating the AI vendors who offer these solutions. Not all AI vendors provide the same level of support, integration flexibility, or industry expertise, so it's essential to choose a vendor that complements the organization's needs and structure.

Vendor Evaluation Criteria:

Industry Experience: Vendors with procurement-specific experience are more likely to understand industry-specific challenges and offer relevant insights.

Scalability: Choose vendors whose AI solutions can grow with the company's needs, accommodating additional users, larger datasets, or expanded functionalities.

Integration Capability: Assess whether the AI tool can seamlessly integrate with existing procurement systems, ERP software, and data sources.

Customer Support and Training: Opt for vendors who provide ongoing support, training sessions, and resources to help users maximize the tool's value.

Data Security and Compliance: Verify that the vendor adheres to industry standards for data security, privacy, and regulatory compliance, especially if handling sensitive supplier information.

Example Vendor Assessment:

For a company handling a large volume of confidential data, a vendor with a strong track record in data security and privacy compliance would be a high priority.

4. Pilot Testing AI Solutions

Before full-scale implementation, conducting a pilot program with a selected AI tool can help validate its effectiveness, identify any unforeseen issues, and ensure team readiness. Pilot testing allows organizations to experience the tool in real-world conditions on a smaller scale, providing insight into potential challenges and areas for adjustment.

Steps for Effective Pilot Testing:

Define Pilot Scope: Choose a specific area within procurement for the pilot, such as demand forecasting or supplier risk assessment, to keep the test manageable.

Set Success Metrics: Identify key performance indicators (KPIs) to measure success, such as time saved, reduction in errors, or improvement in decision-making speed.

Gather User Feedback: Collect feedback from procurement team members using the tool during the pilot to identify areas for improvement or additional training needs.

Evaluate Performance: Compare pilot results with existing benchmarks to assess the tool's value. For example, a successful pilot in spend analytics may show a quantifiable improvement in cost savings or budget allocation accuracy.

5. Implementing AI Solutions in Stages

Implementing an AI tool across the entire procurement function can be disruptive if done all at once. A staged approach allows the team to adapt gradually, gain confidence, and make any necessary adjustments before full deployment.

Phased Implementation Approach:

Stage 1: Core Functionality: Start by implementing core features that address the most pressing needs, such as spend analytics or supplier evaluation.

Stage 2: Secondary Features: Once the team is comfortable with the primary functions, roll out additional features like contract management automation or predictive risk analysis.

Stage 3: Continuous Monitoring and Adjustment: After full implementation, continuously monitor performance and user feedback, refining processes or retraining models as necessary.

Example Phased Implementation:

For a procurement department focused on supplier management, initial implementation might include basic supplier evaluation features, followed by more advanced AI-driven risk assessments and performance tracking in later phases.

6. Training Teams on AI Utilization

Successful AI adoption requires that procurement teams are not only trained in how to use the AI tools but also understand the broader role of AI in supporting strategic decisions. Training should address both technical skills and how to interpret AI insights effectively.

Training Components for Procurement Teams:

Tool Functionality Training: Ensure users know how to use the tool's interface, input data, and retrieve reports.

Data Interpretation Skills: Train procurement professionals on how to interpret AI-driven insights and integrate them into their decision-making.

AI and Data Literacy: Educate team members on basic AI concepts, such as machine learning and predictive analytics, helping them understand the tool's capabilities and limitations.

Continuous Learning Opportunities: Offer ongoing learning sessions or workshops to keep the team updated on new features, best practices, and emerging trends in AI for procurement.

7. Measuring AI Solution Performance

Evaluating the effectiveness of AI tools post-implementation is crucial to ensure they meet the desired objectives and deliver value.

Performance should be measured based on the original goals set during the planning phase, with KPIs tailored to specific procurement needs.

Key Performance Metrics:

Cost Savings: Measure reductions in procurement costs due to spend analytics, supplier optimization, or improved demand forecasting.

Process Efficiency: Track improvements in task completion time, error reduction, and workflow automation.

Supplier Performance: Monitor metrics related to supplier evaluation, including compliance rates, delivery accuracy, and risk levels.

User Satisfaction: Gauge team members' satisfaction with the AI tool and its ease of use to ensure it is contributing positively to the work environment.

Example Performance Monitoring:

A procurement team using AI for contract management might measure success through reduced contract review time, fewer compliance issues, and positive feedback from users regarding efficiency improvements.

8. Continuous Improvement and AI Model Refinement

AI tools, particularly those with machine learning capabilities, require continuous refinement to ensure their models remain accurate and relevant. Regularly updating AI algorithms with fresh data and adjusting parameters based on user feedback are essential to maintaining their effectiveness.

Strategies for Continuous Improvement:

Model Retraining: Regularly retrain AI models using new data to improve prediction accuracy and keep insights relevant.

User Feedback Loops: Implement feedback mechanisms where users can report issues or suggest enhancements, enabling the tool to evolve in line with real-world requirements.

Adjusting Based on KPIs: If certain KPIs are not meeting targets, revisit the model's inputs, parameters, or focus areas to make necessary adjustments.

Staying Informed on Technological Advances: Keep up-to-date with advancements in AI to identify new tools, features, or best practices that could further enhance procurement.

Selecting and implementing AI solutions in procurement is a comprehensive process that requires strategic planning, thoughtful evaluation, and a commitment to continuous improvement. By defining clear objectives, choosing solutions that align with these goals, and implementing them in stages, organizations can effectively harness AI to drive efficiency, cost savings, and strategic value. With the right support, training, and ongoing monitoring, AI has the potential to transform procurement, empowering teams to make data-driven decisions that improve supplier relationships, reduce risk, and optimize spending.

Chapter 22: Integrating AI with ERP and Procurement Systems

The integration of Artificial Intelligence (AI) with existing Enterprise Resource Planning (ERP) and procurement systems is a crucial step toward maximizing the value of AI-driven solutions. This integration not only enhances operational efficiency but also enables organizations to leverage data and insights more effectively across the procurement function. This chapter provides a comprehensive guide on how to successfully merge AI with current systems and workflows, ensuring a smooth transition that supports strategic procurement objectives.

1. Understanding the Importance of Integration

Integrating AI with ERP and procurement systems is essential for several reasons:

Data Synergy: AI systems thrive on data. Integrating AI with existing ERP systems allows for the seamless flow of data, enabling AI to analyze historical trends, spending patterns, and supplier performance.

Improved Decision-Making: By combining AI capabilities with ERP functionalities, organizations can enhance decision-making processes, ensuring they are based on real-time data and predictive insights.

Streamlined Processes: Integration helps eliminate data silos, allowing procurement professionals to work more efficiently and collaborate across departments.

Enhanced User Experience: A unified system can simplify user interfaces and improve access to data, making it easier for procurement teams to utilize AI tools.

2. Assessing Current Systems and Workflows

Before initiating the integration process, it's vital to conduct a thorough assessment of the existing ERP and procurement systems:

Identify Existing Tools: Document the current systems in use, such as ERP platforms, procurement management systems, and any standalone AI tools.

Evaluate System Compatibility: Analyze the compatibility of these systems with potential AI solutions. Identify any technical limitations or requirements for integration.

Map Existing Workflows: Understand how procurement processes currently operate, including data flow, task assignments, and approval processes. This mapping helps pinpoint areas where AI can add value.

3. Defining Integration Goals and Objectives

Clearly defined integration goals are crucial for guiding the process and measuring success. Consider the following objectives:

Enhanced Data Analysis: Aim to improve data analytics capabilities by enabling AI to draw insights from the ERP system's data.

Automation of Routine Tasks: Identify tasks within procurement that can be automated using AI, such as purchase order generation, invoice processing, and supplier evaluations.

Real-Time Insights: Focus on providing procurement teams with real-time insights derived from integrated data, facilitating more informed decision-making.

Seamless User Experience: Strive for a unified interface that allows users to access both ERP and AI functionalities without friction.

4. Selecting the Right AI Solutions for Integration

When choosing AI solutions for integration, it's important to consider compatibility with existing systems. Key factors to evaluate include:

Integration Capabilities: Assess whether the AI tool offers APIs (Application Programming Interfaces) or other integration options that facilitate seamless connectivity with your ERP system.

Customization Options: Look for AI solutions that can be tailored to your specific procurement processes and requirements.

Vendor Support: Choose vendors that offer comprehensive support during the integration process, including training and troubleshooting.

5. Developing an Integration Plan

A detailed integration plan is essential for guiding the process. This plan should include:

Timeline: Establish a clear timeline for the integration process, outlining key milestones and deadlines.

Resource Allocation: Identify the resources needed for integration, including personnel, budget, and technology.

Risk Management: Assess potential risks associated with the integration and develop strategies to mitigate them. This might include planning for data migration challenges or compatibility issues.

6. Implementing the Integration

Once the plan is in place, the actual integration process can begin. This involves several key steps:

Data Mapping and Migration: Ensure that data from the ERP system is accurately mapped to the AI tool. This includes defining data formats, structures, and any necessary transformations. Migrate historical data into the new system to enable effective analysis.

APIs and Connectivity: Set up the necessary APIs or middleware that will enable communication between the AI solution and the ERP system. This may require collaboration with IT teams to ensure proper configuration.

Testing: Conduct rigorous testing of the integrated systems to identify any issues or bottlenecks. Test data flows, user functionalities, and integration performance to ensure everything operates as expected.

7. Training and Change Management

Integrating AI with existing systems will likely require a change in workflows and processes, necessitating a focus on training and change management:

User Training: Provide training sessions for procurement teams on how to utilize the integrated system effectively. Focus on demonstrating the benefits of AI integration and how it enhances their existing workflows.

Change Management Strategies: Implement strategies to manage the transition smoothly. This might include regular updates, feedback loops, and addressing any concerns from users regarding the new system.

8. Continuous Monitoring and Optimization

After the integration is complete, continuous monitoring is essential to ensure that the system is functioning effectively and delivering the expected benefits:

Performance Metrics: Define KPIs to assess the performance of the integrated system, such as user adoption rates, cost savings, and efficiency improvements.

User Feedback: Encourage procurement teams to provide feedback on their experiences with the integrated system. This feedback can highlight areas for improvement or additional training needs.

Iterative Refinement: Based on performance metrics and user feedback, make necessary adjustments to optimize the integration. This could involve refining data workflows, enhancing automation capabilities, or adding new functionalities.

9. Future-Proofing Integration

As technology continues to evolve, organizations should consider future-proofing their integration efforts:

189

Stay Informed on Trends: Keep up with advancements in AI and ERP technologies. Being aware of emerging trends can help organizations adapt their systems and processes accordingly.

Scalability Considerations: Ensure that the integrated system is scalable, capable of accommodating future growth and changes in procurement needs.

Continuous Learning: Foster a culture of continuous learning within the procurement team. Encourage ongoing training and professional development to keep up with technological advancements.

Integrating AI with ERP and procurement systems is a transformative journey that requires careful planning, execution, and ongoing optimization. By understanding current systems, defining clear integration goals, selecting the right AI solutions, and focusing on user training and change management, organizations can successfully merge AI capabilities with their existing workflows. This integration not only enhances procurement efficiency but also empowers teams to make data-driven decisions that drive strategic value. As the landscape of procurement continues to evolve, organizations that prioritize effective integration will position themselves for sustained success in an increasingly competitive environment.

Part 7: The Future of AI and ML in Procurement

Chapter 23: The Potential of Blockchain and AI in Procurement

As organizations strive for efficiency, transparency, and innovation in their procurement processes, the convergence of Artificial Intelligence (AI) and Blockchain technology presents a compelling opportunity. This chapter explores the synergistic potential of these technologies in procurement, examining how they can work together to enhance supply chain operations, increase trust among stakeholders, and drive more informed decision-making.

1. Understanding Blockchain Technology

Blockchain is a decentralized digital ledger that records transactions across multiple computers in a way that the registered information cannot be altered retroactively. This technology is characterized by:

Transparency: All participants in a blockchain network can access the same information, reducing disputes and enhancing trust.

Immutability: Once data is recorded on the blockchain, it cannot be changed without consensus from the network participants, ensuring data integrity.

Decentralization: By eliminating the need for a central authority, blockchain fosters direct peer-to-peer transactions, reducing the risk of fraud and improving security.

In procurement, these features can address various challenges, such as lack of visibility, compliance issues, and fraud.

2. The Role of AI in Procurement

AI technologies, including machine learning, natural language processing, and predictive analytics, are revolutionizing procurement by automating processes, analyzing vast amounts of data, and providing insights that drive strategic decisions. AI applications in procurement can include:

Supplier selection and evaluation: Automating the assessment of suppliers based on performance data, pricing, and risk factors.

Demand forecasting: Utilizing historical data to predict future demand more accurately.

Spend analysis: Analyzing purchasing data to identify cost-saving opportunities.

By leveraging AI, procurement professionals can make data-driven decisions and enhance operational efficiency.

3. The Synergy Between Blockchain and AI

Combining blockchain and AI creates a powerful ecosystem that can address many procurement challenges and enhance supply chain management. This synergy offers several key benefits:

Enhanced Data Integrity: Blockchain's immutability ensures that the data used by AI algorithms is accurate and trustworthy. This integrity is crucial for the effectiveness of AI-driven insights and predictions.

Improved Transparency: AI can analyze data recorded on the blockchain to provide real-time insights into supply chain activities. This transparency helps organizations track transactions, monitor supplier performance, and ensure compliance.

Automated Contract Management: Smart contracts—self-executing contracts with terms directly written into code—can be deployed on blockchain. AI can facilitate contract analysis and execution, automatically triggering actions based on predefined conditions.

4. Use Cases for Blockchain and AI in Procurement

Several practical use cases illustrate how the integration of AI and blockchain can transform procurement:

a. Supplier Verification and Onboarding

Blockchain can store verified supplier credentials, certifications, and performance histories. AI can analyze this data to assess supplier suitability and automate the onboarding process, reducing the time and effort required to validate suppliers.

b. Risk Management and Fraud Detection

AI can analyze transaction patterns recorded on the blockchain to identify anomalies and potential fraud. For example, if a supplier's invoicing deviates significantly from previous transactions, AI can flag this for further investigation. The transparent nature of blockchain allows for real-time tracking of all transactions, enhancing risk mitigation strategies.

c. Smart Contracts for Automated Transactions

Smart contracts can automate payment processes based on conditions agreed upon by the parties involved. AI can be used to evaluate whether these conditions have been met before triggering the payment, streamlining transactions and reducing administrative overhead.

d. Traceability and Provenance

In industries like food and pharmaceuticals, traceability is crucial. Blockchain can provide an immutable record of every step in the supply chain, while AI can analyze this data to ensure compliance with regulations and identify potential issues. For example, AI can assess whether products have been stored and transported under the right conditions based on the data recorded on the blockchain.

5. Challenges and Considerations

While the integration of AI and blockchain in procurement offers significant potential, several challenges must be addressed:

Complexity and Cost: Implementing blockchain technology can be complex and costly. Organizations must carefully assess the return on investment before embarking on integration efforts.

Interoperability: For blockchain to be effective in procurement, it must be compatible with existing systems and technologies. Ensuring interoperability between various platforms is essential for success.

Data Privacy and Security: While blockchain enhances data integrity, concerns about data privacy and security must be considered. Organizations must establish protocols to protect sensitive information while leveraging the benefits of blockchain.

Change Management: The shift to AI and blockchain technologies may require significant changes in organizational processes and employee roles. Effective change management strategies are essential to ensure a smooth transition.

6. The Future Outlook

The combination of AI and blockchain in procurement is still in its early stages, but its potential is immense. As organizations increasingly recognize the benefits of these technologies, we can expect to see:

Wider Adoption: More organizations will begin to adopt AI and blockchain solutions in procurement, leading to a more standardized approach to supply chain management.

Innovation in Smart Contracts: The use of smart contracts will become more sophisticated, incorporating advanced AI algorithms to enhance contract management and execution.

Data-Driven Decision-Making: Procurement teams will increasingly rely on AI-driven insights derived from blockchain data to inform strategic decisions.

Enhanced Collaboration: As transparency improves through blockchain, collaboration among stakeholders will become more effective, fostering trust and enhancing supply chain relationships.

The integration of AI and blockchain technology in procurement represents a significant evolution in how organizations manage their supply chains. By leveraging the strengths of both technologies, organizations can enhance data integrity, improve transparency, automate processes, and make more informed decisions. While challenges exist, the potential benefits far outweigh the obstacles. As the landscape of procurement continues to evolve, embracing the synergy between AI and blockchain will be crucial for organizations seeking to stay competitive in an increasingly complex and dynamic marketplace.

Chapter 24: Ethics and Data Privacy in AI Procurement

As procurement increasingly adopts Artificial Intelligence (AI) technologies, it raises essential ethical and data privacy considerations. The integration of AI can bring efficiencies and insights, but it also poses challenges related to fairness, transparency, accountability, and the protection of sensitive data. This chapter explores the ethical implications and data privacy concerns surrounding AI in procurement, along with strategies to navigate these issues responsibly.

1. The Importance of Ethics in AI Procurement

Ethics in AI procurement is paramount for several reasons:

Trust and Reputation: Organizations must cultivate trust among stakeholders, including suppliers, employees, and customers. Ethical AI practices can enhance an organization's reputation and foster strong relationships.

Compliance: Many countries and regions have enacted laws and regulations governing data privacy and AI usage. Adhering to these regulations is essential for avoiding legal repercussions and ensuring ethical standards.

Sustainability and Social Responsibility: Ethical AI practices contribute to sustainability goals and social responsibility, aligning procurement strategies with broader organizational values.

2. Key Ethical Considerations

Several ethical issues arise when implementing AI in procurement:

a. Fairness and Bias

AI systems are only as unbiased as the data they are trained on. If historical data reflects biases—whether related to race, gender, or socioeconomic status—these biases can be perpetuated in AI decision-making. For example, if an AI model evaluates suppliers based on past performance data that disproportionately favors certain demographics, it could reinforce systemic inequalities.

Strategies to Mitigate Bias:

Conduct regular audits of AI algorithms to identify and address biases.

Use diverse datasets that accurately represent the supplier landscape.

Involve multidisciplinary teams in the development of AI systems to ensure diverse perspectives are considered.

b. Transparency and Explainability

AI systems often operate as "black boxes," making it challenging to understand how decisions are made. In procurement, this lack of transparency can lead to mistrust among stakeholders. Suppliers may feel aggrieved if they are evaluated unfavorably without understanding the rationale behind the decision.

Strategies to Enhance Transparency:

Develop explainable AI models that can articulate the factors influencing decisions.

Provide clear communication to suppliers about how AI tools are used in the evaluation process.

Implement feedback mechanisms that allow suppliers to seek clarification on decisions made by AI systems.

c. Accountability

As organizations increasingly rely on AI for procurement decisions, determining accountability for those decisions becomes complex. If an AI system makes an erroneous decision that impacts a supplier negatively, identifying who is responsible—the AI developer, the procurement team, or the organization—can be challenging.

Strategies to Establish Accountability:

Clearly define roles and responsibilities related to AI implementation and decision-making.

Establish governance frameworks that outline accountability measures for AI-driven decisions.

Document the decision-making processes and criteria used in AI systems to facilitate accountability.

3. Data Privacy Concerns in AI Procurement

The use of AI in procurement often requires the collection, storage, and analysis of vast amounts of data, including sensitive supplier and transaction information. This raises significant data privacy concerns:

a. Data Security

Ensuring the security of procurement data is paramount to prevent unauthorized access and data breaches. Such incidents can lead to severe reputational and financial consequences.

Strategies to Enhance Data Security:

Implement robust cybersecurity measures, including encryption, access controls, and regular security audits.

Train employees on data privacy and security best practices to minimize the risk of human error.

Conduct regular assessments of data security protocols to adapt to emerging threats.

b. Consent and Data Ownership

Organizations must ensure that they have the appropriate consent to collect and use supplier data. Additionally, questions around data ownership arise: who owns the data generated through AI systems, and how can it be used?

Strategies for Managing Data Ownership and Consent:

Clearly communicate data collection practices and obtain explicit consent from suppliers.

Establish data-sharing agreements that outline ownership, usage rights, and limitations.

Be transparent about how supplier data will be used in AI models and decision-making processes.

c. Compliance with Regulations

Many jurisdictions have implemented strict data privacy regulations, such as the General Data Protection Regulation (GDPR) in Europe and the California Consumer Privacy Act (CCPA) in the United States. Organizations must navigate these regulations to ensure compliance.

Strategies for Regulatory Compliance:

Stay informed about relevant data privacy laws and their implications for AI in procurement.

Conduct regular compliance audits to ensure adherence to data protection regulations.

Implement data management practices that align with regulatory requirements.

4. Best Practices for Ethical AI Procurement

To navigate the ethical and data privacy challenges associated with AI procurement, organizations can adopt the following best practices:

Establish an Ethical Framework: Create a framework that outlines the ethical principles guiding AI use in procurement, addressing fairness, transparency, and accountability.

Engage Stakeholders: Involve suppliers, employees, and other stakeholders in discussions about AI implementation to gain diverse perspectives and foster collaboration.

Invest in Training and Education: Provide training on AI ethics and data privacy for procurement teams to ensure they understand the implications of their decisions.

Regularly Review AI Systems: Conduct ongoing evaluations of AI algorithms and models to assess their fairness, accuracy, and compliance with ethical standards.

5. The Role of Leadership in Ethical AI Procurement

Leadership plays a crucial role in fostering an ethical culture around AI procurement. Executives and managers should:

Set the Tone at the Top: Demonstrate a commitment to ethical AI practices through transparent communication and policy enforcement.

Allocate Resources: Invest in the necessary tools, training, and technology to implement ethical AI procurement practices.

Encourage a Culture of Accountability: Foster an environment where employees feel empowered to voice concerns about ethical dilemmas related to AI.

The integration of AI in procurement holds immense potential for enhancing efficiency, transparency, and decision-making. However, it also presents significant ethical and data privacy challenges that organizations must address proactively. By implementing best practices, engaging stakeholders, and fostering a culture of accountability, organizations can navigate these challenges responsibly. Ultimately, prioritizing ethics and data privacy in AI procurement will build trust among stakeholders and contribute to sustainable, responsible business practices.

Chapter 25: Future Trends and Innovations in Procurement Technology

The procurement landscape is undergoing a transformative shift due to advancements in Artificial Intelligence (AI) and Machine Learning (ML). As these technologies evolve, they promise to enhance efficiency, drive innovation, and redefine the role of procurement within organizations. This chapter explores future trends and innovations in procurement technology, emphasizing the anticipated impact of AI and ML on procurement processes and practices.

1. Enhanced Predictive Analytics

Predictive analytics is set to become a cornerstone of procurement decision-making. As AI and ML algorithms become more sophisticated, they will enable organizations to forecast demand, identify supplier risks, and optimize inventory levels with greater accuracy.

Demand Forecasting: Advanced predictive analytics will harness data from multiple sources—historical sales data, market trends, weather forecasts, and social media sentiment—to improve demand planning. By anticipating shifts in demand, procurement teams can better align their strategies with organizational goals, reducing excess inventory and minimizing stockouts.

Supplier Risk Assessment: AI will facilitate real-time risk assessments of suppliers by analyzing financial stability, operational performance, and geopolitical factors. This proactive approach will empower organizations to mitigate risks before they impact supply chains, ensuring continuity and resilience.

2. Autonomous Procurement Systems

The future of procurement will witness the emergence of autonomous systems that can operate with minimal human intervention. These systems will leverage AI and ML to automate routine tasks, enabling procurement professionals to focus on strategic activities.

Automated Purchase Orders: AI-driven systems will autonomously generate purchase orders based on predefined criteria, historical data, and real-time inventory levels. This automation will reduce manual errors and improve efficiency, allowing procurement teams to respond swiftly to changing business needs.

Intelligent Contract Management: Smart contracts powered by AI will automatically execute terms and conditions based on predefined criteria. These contracts will reduce the need for manual intervention, streamline compliance, and enhance transparency in supplier relationships.

3. Integration of Blockchain Technology

Blockchain technology is poised to revolutionize procurement by providing a secure, transparent, and tamper-proof record of transactions. When combined with AI and ML, blockchain can enhance traceability, accountability, and trust in the procurement process.

Supplier Transparency: Blockchain will enable organizations to verify the authenticity of suppliers and their products. By providing a transparent record of the supply chain, procurement teams can ensure compliance with ethical and sustainability standards, fostering trust among stakeholders.

Streamlined Payments: Smart contracts on blockchain networks can automate payment processes, reducing the time and cost associated with traditional payment methods. This efficiency will enhance supplier relationships and improve cash flow management.

4. AI-Driven Supplier Relationship Management

The future of procurement will see a shift from transactional relationships to collaborative partnerships, facilitated by AI-driven supplier relationship management (SRM) systems. These systems will leverage data analytics to enhance communication, performance monitoring, and strategic alignment.

Personalized Engagement: AI will analyze supplier data to provide insights into their performance, preferences, and needs. This personalization will enable procurement teams to tailor their engagement strategies, fostering stronger relationships and collaboration.

Performance Optimization: AI-driven SRM systems will continuously monitor supplier performance metrics, identifying areas for improvement and providing actionable insights. This proactive approach will enhance supplier performance, leading to better quality, reduced costs, and improved service levels.

5. Sustainability and Ethical Procurement

As organizations increasingly prioritize sustainability and ethical practices, AI and ML will play a crucial role in supporting these initiatives. Procurement technology will enable organizations to assess the environmental and social impact of their sourcing decisions.

Sustainable Supplier Selection: AI will facilitate the evaluation of suppliers based on sustainability criteria, such as carbon footprint, labor practices, and resource usage. This capability will empower procurement teams to make informed decisions that align with organizational sustainability goals.

Lifecycle Assessment: Advanced analytics will allow organizations to conduct lifecycle assessments of products, identifying opportunities for waste reduction, recycling, and sustainable sourcing. By integrating sustainability into procurement strategies, organizations can enhance their reputation and meet regulatory requirements.

6. The Rise of Augmented Intelligence

While AI will automate many procurement processes, the future will also see the rise of augmented intelligence—combining human expertise with AI capabilities. This hybrid approach will enhance decision-making, creativity, and innovation in procurement.

Collaborative Decision-Making: AI-powered tools will provide procurement professionals with data-driven insights, enabling them to make informed decisions while leveraging their domain expertise. This collaboration will lead to more innovative solutions and better outcomes.

Continuous Learning: ML algorithms will evolve through continuous learning from user interactions and market trends. This adaptability will enhance the accuracy and relevance of AI-driven recommendations, enabling procurement teams to stay agile and responsive.

7. Advanced Data Management and Integration

As procurement technology evolves, organizations will need robust data management strategies to harness the full potential of AI and ML. Advanced data integration platforms will enable seamless data flow between procurement systems and other enterprise applications.

Unified Data Ecosystem: Organizations will create a unified data ecosystem that consolidates procurement data from various sources, including ERP systems, supplier databases, and market intelligence platforms. This holistic view will empower procurement teams to make data-driven decisions and uncover new opportunities.

Data Governance: Effective data governance frameworks will ensure data quality, security, and compliance with regulations. Organizations will need to establish clear policies and practices for data management, ensuring that AI and ML algorithms operate on accurate and reliable data.

8. Enhanced User Experience through AI

The user experience in procurement will undergo significant improvements as AI technologies enhance user interfaces and interactions. Procurement professionals will benefit from intuitive tools that streamline workflows and provide actionable insights.

Natural Language Processing (NLP): NLP will enable procurement teams to interact with AI systems using natural language, making it easier to retrieve information, generate reports, and ask questions. This user-friendly approach will reduce the learning curve and enhance productivity.

Intelligent Assistants: AI-powered virtual assistants will support procurement professionals by providing real-time insights, reminders, and recommendations. These assistants will enhance efficiency and allow procurement teams to focus on strategic initiatives.

9. Continuous Adaptation to Market Dynamics

The pace of change in the procurement landscape is accelerating, driven by technological advancements and evolving market dynamics. Organizations must remain agile and adaptive to leverage the benefits of AI and ML effectively.

Agile Procurement Processes: AI technologies will enable organizations to adopt agile procurement processes that respond swiftly to changing market conditions. By leveraging real-time data and analytics, procurement teams can make informed decisions and adjust strategies as needed.

Scenario Planning: Advanced analytics will support scenario planning, allowing procurement teams to simulate various market conditions and assess the potential impact on sourcing strategies. This capability will enhance resilience and prepare organizations for uncertainty.

The future of procurement technology is bright, with AI and ML set to drive significant advancements and innovations. From enhanced predictive analytics to autonomous systems, organizations that embrace these technologies will gain a competitive edge. By prioritizing transparency, collaboration, and sustainability, procurement teams can leverage the full potential of AI and ML, transforming procurement into a strategic driver of organizational success. As the landscape evolves, organizations must remain adaptable and proactive, harnessing emerging technologies to navigate the complexities of modern procurement effectively.